Art and the Message of the Church

Westminster Studies in Christian Communication
Kendig Brubaker Cully, General Editor

Art
and the Message
of the Church

WALTER L. NATHAN

THE WESTMINSTER PRESS
Philadelphia

To my wife
(Prov. 31:28-29)

Contents

A Note on Westminster Studies
in Christian Communication

These Studies are predicated on the ground that the Christian faith needs to be made relevant to persons in the modern world in terms of the dynamic nature of the faith itself and the channels that are capable of conveying such a faith. In itself any technique of communication conceivably could serve as well for secular as for religious ends. In this series a wide variety of means and methods of communication will be analyzed in the light of their availability to, and suitability for, the particular tasks that the Christian church faces in bringing the realities of faith to bear upon the life of actual persons in the contemporary situation.

Oftentimes in the past, techniques have been viewed almost as ends in themselves. Or, they have been taken over uncritically from the secular culture without being subjected to adequate scrutiny as to whether they are appropriate for the church's use. On the other hand, sometimes the church has been blind to the life situations of the present to such an extent as to ignore the real ways in which people's lives are influenced by all that impinges on them. In the latter case, the church has failed to bring the life-giving power of the gospel to bear on contemporary culture because of a lack of understanding of, or appreciation for, the means of communication that have been proved capable of changing lives and societies.

Involving as it does both the " What " and the " How," the whole question of the communication of the gospel in the modern world is pivotal in the present juncture of history. The present Studies will be aimed at bringing the " What " and the " How " together fruitfully. These books are designed to make a contribution to the ongoing conversations across boundaries.

Theology, Biblical studies, sociology, cultural anthropology, psychology, education, art, letters, science, and the other disciplines all have something to say to one another. In our present concern, " communication " refers to the way in which the Christian faith can come into conjunction with what is happening in the total world of life and ideas in the middle decades of the twentieth century. In each of these Studies attention will focus on some important aspect of the basic question: How can the church most effectively preach, teach, and otherwise manifest the gospel in the growing edges of man's present-day culture? No aspect of man's actual situation is alien to such a question. No medium of communication should fail to come under scrutiny if, as Christians, we are eager to have the Word of God confront a confused generation powerfully and compellingly.

Each volume in Westminster Studies in Christian Communication will be an authentic voice of one perceptive interpreter. No effort has been made to suggest to any writer what " line " he ought to follow. Each work will be adjudged by the readers on its own merits. The writers themselves conceivably might disagree heartily with regard to certain presuppositions or conclusions held by their colleagues. All this will be to the good if the result of these Studies should be the stimulating of many conversations. Yet all the writers have in mind a focus that is realistic, an emphasis that is practical, and a discussion that is timely. The only request made of the authors is that they speak out of their knowledge to the very heart and mind of our times. Depth without dullness, breadth without diffuseness, challenge without sentimentality — these, at least, it is hoped, will be characteristics of all the Studies. We are grateful to those who have consented to share in this venture into communication, and we commend their work as in itself an integral part of the church's task of communication.

KENDIG BRUBAKER CULLY
General Editor

Evanston, Illinois

REQUIESCAT IN PACE

Little did we know, when arrangements for this book were completed, that Walter L. Nathan, its author, would be fatally stricken even before he could see its proofs. His death on May 19, 1961, destroyed our hope that still further significant writing would follow ART AND THE MESSAGE OF THE CHURCH. This study, therefore, becomes his testament of faith and a witness to his personal " confrontation with the ultimate problem of all existence," to use his own words from this book.

K. B. C.

Introduction

Where We Stand

 *A poet, a painter, a musician, an architect,
the man or woman who is not one of these
is not a Christian.*

— William Blake.

Several years ago one of America's foremost sculptors was
planning to move from New York City to the Southwest. He
had in his studio the over-life-size model of a figure of Christ,
an unusually fine work in simple, heroic forms, modern without being " radical." He had hoped for some time to receive a
commission to carve it in enduring stone, perhaps for a place
where it could speak of peace and neighborly love, like the
Christ of the Andes. Yet the artist's efforts and those of his
friends had proved fruitless.

Time was running short. Rather than put the large statue in
storage, the artist wished to give it to one of the many churches
in New York for safekeeping and exhibition, and asked only
that the church pay the cost of moving it. A leading church-
man came to see the " Christ," and, greatly impressed, tried his
best to find a home for it. It was in vain. The statue had to be
stored away. The saddened sculptor consoled himself with
the thought that when Christ was an infant they could not find
a place for him either except in a manger.

The incident is by no means unique. Many a sculptor and
painter has discovered that the churches are apparently not
interested in living religious art. The very people to whom its

13

message was addressed were not listening or did not care. The artists had to consider themselves fortunate if a private collector or a museum acquired the work they had meant for a place of Christian worship, a church school, or a pastor's study.

The indifference of the churches toward the visual arts of our time is not just a phenomenon of American life. The French painter Georges Rouault had earned world-wide respect among laymen and art critics long before he was given his first opportunity to work for a church in his country. Most of his religious paintings are in private or public collections.

Museums, however, buy works of art for aesthetic, not spiritual, reasons. When a religious painting is exhibited side by side with works of an entirely different character, it is primarily seen as an example of a given style or period and loses its full significance. Occasionally, a museum can assign a room to a single masterpiece. Raphael's *Sistine Madonna* in Dresden, his *Betrothal of Mary* in Milan, are cases in point. The *Avignon Pieta,* by an unknown French painter of the fifteenth century, has at least a wall by itself in the Louvre, and there are a few other examples. Obviously, public art collections can do so only in rare instances, and this cannot be considered an ideal solution. For even arrangements of this kind tend to emphasize the outstanding fame of the painting, its importance in the history of art, rather than its religious message.

Of course, no one would wish to suggest that museums should not exhibit works of religious content. During long periods of history very little else was produced. And since much of Christian art of the past no longer carries a living message for our time, works of this nature are best preserved in museums. This practice also has the advantage of bringing together works that have been widely scattered, sometimes in all but inaccessible places. We can rejoice that the great masterpieces of art have now become available in good color reproductions, but to see the originals well displayed in a museum is to be much preferred.

What causes serious concern is the neglect of religious art, in particular that of our own time, on the part of many churches. Either they show little or no awareness of the spiritual values of art and its function in the service of God, or are satisfied with a weak echo of the past, often trying to make up in sumptuousness what is lacking in vitality. Far too often they cling to an outdated, stereotyped "popular" kind of religious art that is characterized by anemic correctness and sugar-coated sentimentality. Commercial suppliers reprint the same pictures year after year, and sell them despite their rejection by every informed critic, Protestant as well as Roman Catholic. It is undoubtedly easier, and involves less financial risk, to repeat what is known to be widely accepted than to offer something new and better. Besides, some loyal Christians have been so thoroughly conditioned to this type of "devotionals" as to react with hostility against anything unfamiliar, whether old or new. These church members usually make their views prevail, the more so since very few clergymen are equipped for leadership in the field of art. As a result, the standard of artistic taste in the churches has in many cases remained at the level of almost a century ago.

But the "popular" kind of religious art has long since lost whatever power to move and inspire it may once have had, at least as far as the younger generation is concerned. With notable and fortunately increasing exceptions, the churches have remained static in an area where they ought to be courageously leading. As bearers of a timeless message they are by nature inclined to be conservative, slow to give up traditional patterns even after such have become merely dead forms. Yet they cannot fulfill the command to "go into all the world and preach the gospel to the whole creation" (Mark 16:15) if they are content to stand still. Today, as in Paul's time, the gospel can be preached in meaningful ways only by men who are "sent," who are prepared to go and speak to the people where the people are.

One of the remarkable aspects of modern living is the degree to which we depend on visual communication. Countless im-

ages enter our consciousness day in and day out, through newspapers, magazines, billboards, the movies, and television. Much
of this vast flood is merely distracting or rushes by unheeded,
though recent motivational research has disclosed how subtly
it can influence our thinking. Now and then we are arrested by
a forceful image. Outstanding photographs such as those gathered for the exhibition "The Family of Man" (Museum of
Modern Art, New York, 1955) have left on many viewers here
and abroad an impact more profound than any number of
written or spoken words. Political and social campaigns and,
of course, commercial advertising rely heavily on the effective
presentation of carefully chosen visual materials.

In addition, the publication in journals of mass distribution
of great works of art of both the past and the present, formerly
known only to the few, has already affected the thinking of
large groups of people. Editors are confident of a favorable response to those presentations, which in turn stimulate a growing interest. Beautifully illustrated art books find a much wider
market than ever before and of late have become available in
inexpensive paper-bound editions. Museums and galleries are
being established in numerous communities where none had
existed, and, like their older sisters, welcome ever-larger numbers of visitors, old and young. Open-air exhibits of paintings,
sculpture, and architectural designs, such as the annual Arts
Festival in Boston, attract thousands of interested people, and
it is noteworthy how frequently one can spot the little red
symbol marking a sale. Art schools are crowded with hopeful
students; the art departments of practically every college and
university have had to expand greatly to accommodate the
heavy enrollment in courses in art history and appreciation as
well as in studio work. All of these are clear signs of a change
in the atmosphere, of real promise for the cultural life of
the nation.

Another sign is the new enthusiasm for active participation
in an art or craft as a "creative hobby." When modern artists
rediscovered the value of direct, spontaneous expression and

freed themselves from the rules of exact representation and imitation dominant since the time of the Renaissance, they taught us to see the beauty of the art of primitive tribes, of untutored or "folk" painters and carvers, and of the child. Grandma Moses' fame has encouraged men and women of every age group and station in life to follow her example. They are not only finding satisfaction in their creative efforts but, in the process, have become far more open to great art of every period and civilization. We can welcome these activities the more wholeheartedly as they help solve two major problems of our society: how the worker can make productive use of his leisure hours at the end of a day that leaves him fatigued rather than physically exhausted; and how he can retain a zest for living during the years of retirement and the evening of life.

The new interest in the arts reflects, to a degree, a desire to escape from the frustrations, the anxieties, and the bewildering complexities of modern living, a reaction against monotonous routine work in home, office, or factory. In a positive sense, however, it indicates a strong desire for self-realization, for wholeness of personality. Amidst the countless machine-made objects in our environment the work of art, or of craft, constitutes the only truly personal product made from beginning to end by an individual according to his own choice, taste, and ability. In art and craftsmanship man feels free, not "other-directed." When he holds in his hand what he alone has willed into being, he stands happily content on an island of meaning in a sea of meaninglessness. His work releases in him well-springs of energy and joy that the most perfectly shaped, mass-produced object cannot arouse. Having poured his love into the making, he is the richer for it. Those who have not themselves taken up a "creative hobby" can share, through empathy, some of the maker's experience when they acquire original paintings, drawings, prints, ceramics, or any other handmade furnishing. This explains, at least in part, the wide appeal of "antiques." Anything well made by human hands has personal, which means *spiritual,* value in our mechanized era far beyond its price in dollars and cents. Many Americans who once considered art a luxury scarcely worth their attention have come to accept it as a significant factor in their lives.

Continued indifference on the part of the churches could therefore lead only to further estrangement and might very well cause persons sensitive to aesthetic values to place these in the center of their spiritual concerns, where faith rightfully belongs — in other words, to substitute art for religion. At the same time, the much greater response of the people to the arts offers new approaches for the proclamation of the message of Christ, and church leaders of practically every denomination are beginning to become alert to them. In our country and abroad a vigorous new church architecture has stirred up healthy debate; striking modern churches have attracted considerable attention and have become widely known. Gifted sculptors, painters, and workers in the crafts use the artistic language of our time with true conviction to create works of a Christian nature. Exhibitions of contemporary Christian art are no longer unusual events and have been successfully organized by local churches or church councils. The journals of the denominations are far more open to new endeavors and have devoted articles or entire issues to religious art. The National Council of the Churches of Christ in the U.S.A. has set up a Department of Worship and the Arts, while in Roman Catholic circles the Liturgical Arts Society, long a lonely pioneer, is steadily gaining influence. Without realizing it, we may stand at the threshold of a new day for Christian art.

These trends ask for serious consideration. What spiritual values in the visual arts justify granting them a more significant place in the life of the church? What is our artistic heritage? What are the functions of the arts in relation to the message of the church for our time? What principles of selection can be applied? How can we bring art and the church of Christ closer together?

The following chapters are intended, not to provide definitive answers, but to introduce some of the problems involved and to encourage interest and discussion. Our concern is not " art for art's sake," but the conviction that art can help our age toward a deeper awareness of Christian faith, hope, and love. This can bless those who are searching for God because they need him, and those too who " need him even more because they do not yet search for him."

Chapter I

Spiritual Foundations
of the Arts

This is the only means there is to ascend toward God; namely, to do as our Divine Master himself does: to create.
— Paul Gauguin.

A. The Artist as Maker

Man's restless mind is constantly seeking for answers to the fundamental questions of being. In philosophy he inquires about himself and his understanding of the world; in the sciences he tries to wrest from the phenomena of nature the secrets of their functional order. In the arts man accepts himself, his joys and sorrows, and sings praise and thanksgiving. Seen in the light of the Christian faith, the arts can become pathways to his "chief and highest end," which, as the Westminster Catechism states, is "to glorify God, and fully to enjoy him forever." Their endlessly varied manifestations spring from spiritual foundations linked in many ways to those of faith. "Art itself goes spontaneously to God," Jacques Maritain has said, — "to God as the universal principle of all form and all clarity. From the moment it reaches in its own line a certain level of greatness and purity, art heralds without understanding them the invisible order and glory of which all beauty is but a sign; Chinese or Egyptian, it is already Christian, in hope and in symbol." [1]

A charming old fable ascribes the invention of painting to a

maid of Corinth who was saddened by the impending depar-
ture of her beloved for a distant country. As they spent their
last evening together she saw the lamplight cast his shadow on
the wall. Suddenly an inspiration came to her. Taking a piece
of charcoal from the hearth, she traced the outline and thereby
preserved a lasting memory of his presence. The poetic story
points to a deep truth: all true art is the fruit of love; neither
indifference nor hatred possesses the power to create.

Art, like love, is an expression of personality at its most intensive level of involvement. Both require the ability to conceive and the willingness to nourish and shelter the seed of
the future through a period of slow, hidden growth beset with
grave dangers, until it ripens and can see the light of day. A
mother smiles on her newborn child with feelings of mingled
pride and gratitude similar to those of the artist contemplating
his finished work. In such moments of fulfillment we sense that
reason alone cannot fathom the mystery of creation. We feel
ourselves as a link in an endless chain reaching to the origin,
to God. Our small and limited experience opens to us the
meaning of the great truth: " God is love, and he who abides in
love abides in God, and God abides in him " (I John 4:16).

Artist and craftsman are alike in their complete dedication
to the work, their loving identification with it. They also need
to develop the Christian virtues of faith, hope, courage, pa-
tience, and humility in order to accomplish what they have set
out to do. Written on their hearts is Jesus' warning: " No one
who puts his hand to the plow and looks back is fit for the
kingdom of God " (Luke 9:62). But qualities of character are
not enough; these must be joined to the power to create. What
precisely constitutes this power, whence it arises, we do not
know. Neither the laws of evolution nor those of heredity can
adequately explain it, much less those of chance. Mere force
of will cannot produce it; money does not buy it. It is a spiritual force, and by affirming the spirit it presents a stumbling
block to any purely materialistic or causal interpretation of life.
Creativity lifts man to the stature of maker and leads him

inescapably to the recognition of God, the Creator of all. Did not God himself seal this kinship when he chose the lowly home of a craftsman to reveal himself in the person of Jesus Christ?

Creative power at its highest peak we call genius. As the voice of God has always been audible only to the chosen few, the "inspired," so genius is rare among men. Like the prophet, the man of genius walks alone, too far ahead of his fellow men for easy communion. The Romans called the poet *vates*, the seer, and believed him capable of penetrating the veils of the future. Genius is both a blessing and a curse; it possesses its owner, as James Russell Lowell remarked, instead of being possessed by him, as is talent. We admire it in an uneasy way, or it may disturb us to the point of hostile reaction. The man of genius and the prophet alike are always in danger of being cast out, stoned, or crucified. Yet almost every human life knows rare flashes of insight when, for the span of a heartbeat, we too are inspired, when "intimations of immortality" flash lightninglike into our consciousness and we feel able to touch the infinite and to see, for once, not as in a mirror dimly but face to face. While our only response may be silence or tears, the creative artist finds in himself the strength to speak. His work reveals to us with clarity and finality the emotion whose vehemence left us mute, the truth that our groping thought was unable to reach.

To the man of genius, as to the prophet of God, the coming of the creative spirit is often like a whirlwind or a fire shaking him to the foundations of his being. His soul stretches out until its wings touch the ultimate sources of life. "Does not the work of art originate the moment I become aware of my union with the universe?" asked the German painter Philipp Otto Runge. Emerson said, "The artist . . . must work in the spirit in which we conceive a prophet to speak, or an angel of the Lord to act; that is, he is not to speak his own words, or do his own works, or think his own thoughts, but he is to be the organ through which the universal mind acts." [2] And Nicolas Berdyaev spoke of the "eschatological" element in creative power that stems from discontent with the world as it is and aims at replacing it with something better. It "anticipates the transfiguration of the world. This is the meaning of art, of art of any kind. . . . Human creative power is not human only, it is divine-human." He could therefore state, "All the great creative works of man enter into the Kingdom of God."[3]

The man of genius is humble, because he knows himself as the instrument on whose strings a greater hand plays. Inspiration comes as the unexpected, inexplicable gift of grace; his own responsibility is to bring forth the message entrusted to him. Yet all the time he is painfully aware of the distance between vision and work. Michelangelo, at the zenith of his fame, honored by the great and the mighty and envied by his fellow artists, consumed himself in despair over his inability to render the incomparable grandeur of what he saw within him. Every creative mind has to go through dark hours of doubt. Beethoven once wrote: "The true artist knows no pride; he sees that art has no limits. He is dimly aware of how far he is from his goal, and while he is perhaps being admired by others, he grieves that he has not yet reached out where his genius shines like a distant sun." Dissatisfaction leads some artists to continuous toil, even to the destruction of what they had achieved. Others feel compelled to make scores of preliminary efforts before taking the final "leap." Inspiration may end abruptly and leave tantalizing fragments such as Leonardo da Vinci's *Adoration of the Kings* in Florence, or Coleridge's "Kubla Khan." An artist may become the helpless slave of his vision, unable to master it. The American painter Washington Allston was at the height of his career when the idea for the large painting, *Belshazzar's Feast*, struck him with great force. He spent years of work on it, but, unequal to the task, never finished the project. In the end it became on obsession and left him bitterly frustrated.

The great artist knows the need for unremitting self-criticism. Untruths, weaknesses, short cuts, may be invisible to others: to him they are a constant reproach. His workman's experience has proved to him how right Jesus was when he said, "Nothing is hid that shall not be made manifest, nor anything secret that shall not be known and come to light" (Luke 8:17). Nor will he be able to achieve true greatness unless he is ready for change and growth. Rembrandt's early success and popularity did not persuade him to rest content with his achievements and exploit his fame by easy repetition of an accepted formula. On the contrary, we see him mature from year to year and extend his command of color and form until his last paintings, shimmering in an almost unearthly light, reveal depths of the human soul before which we stand in awe.

With a touch of humor the Japanese painter Hokousai explained, at the age of seventy-five: "From the age of six I had a mania for drawing the form of things. By the time I was fifty I had published an infinity of designs, but all I have produced before the age of seventy is not worth considering. At seventy-three I began to understand the real structure of nature, animals, plants, trees, birds, fishes, and insects. Consequently, when I am eighty I shall have made still more progress; at ninety I shall penetrate the mystery of things; at a hundred I shall certainly have reached a marvelous stage, and when I am a hundred and ten everything I do, be it but a dot or a line, will be alive." [4]

Rarely have the great creative artists received the encouragement they deserved. More often we begin to praise great men only after they have died. The history of art shows many instances of neglect or open hostility; artist and prophet alike are frequently without honor in their own country. Now and then a man of genius purposely has hidden his best powers under the guise of attractive talent in order to find recognition, though posterity will regret his selling his birthright for the sake of wealth and fame. As a rule, however, the great artists have refused to compromise with popular demands. They were willing to make real sacrifices in order to remain faithful to the inner voice that told them to state in their own manner what

had experienced and how they saw the world, regardless
ether their time was ready for it or not. To the majority of
their contemporaries their works then appeared cryptic or
meaningless, fit objects for scorn or ridicule. The tragic fate
of Vincent van Gogh is a well-known instance from the recent
past. Less than thirty years after he died in despair, his rejected paintings were acclaimed as masterpieces.

The work of art grows from the overpowering urge to witness
to an experience, an emotion, or insight, and lives only if and
when it is shared by others. Like love, art increases in the giving and taking. While struggling to express his vision, the artist
may cry out with Jacob, " I will not let you go, unless you bless
me." From such heroic effort stems the commanding need for
communication. " Did I search for the way so painfully unless
to show it to the brothers? " Goethe asked. Only as he communicates his message can the artist receive the response he
needs. Without it his creative gifts may wither and die. He is
willing to face opposition, even hatred, but complete lack of
response is stifling. With all his heart he longs not so much for
appreciation, though like every human being he is grateful for
it, as for eyes and minds open to what he has to say. Faith in
his truth sustains him in the years of waiting for this response.
As did the prophet, he would bless those who see and hear.

Art relates to faith also in regard to the dimension of time.
The Judaeo-Christian faith is based in part on the concept of
God as eternal, unchanging, above time:

> Before the mountains were brought forth,
>> or ever thou hadst formed the earth and the world,
>> from everlasting to everlasting thou art God.
>>> (Ps. 90:2.)

But man is bound to time, his greatest enemy. Forever it takes
from him; forever it eludes his grasp. Perhaps art began when
men first became aware that it overcomes time. When an experience has congealed into a work of art, it lives on with an immediacy surpassing the keenest memory and enables us to live

through it again and again. Art builds bridges between past, present, and future. Visitors to prehistoric caves have mentioned an eerie feeling of vanquished time, as if the ancient people had just laid down their tools and might come back any minute. A psalm written three thousand years ago, a centuries-old Chinese scroll, a Bach fugue, can speak as poignantly to those who are sensitive to their greatness as if they had just been created.

To conquer time and remain in the fullest sense alive, that is, capable of evoking in others a vital response and of " speaking to their condition," the work of art must have grown from the very center of the artist's being. It is not enough for him to paint what he sees before him; unless he also paints " what he sees in himself," he will remain timebound. His work, be it ever so skillfully done, will soon fade into an example of an obsolete style to be studied by the art historian much as dried flowers in a herbarium are studied by the botanist, though even then a faint whisper of life will be audible to the observer of a later day. What man's hand and mind have created in love never dies entirely. In the work of art lies an answer to man's longing for freedom from the fetters of time, his wish to make the moment last. It resolves at least in part the conflict between man's awareness of his own finitude and his aspiration toward the infinite. It helps him to understand something of the meaning of God's eternity. Rainer Maria Rilke expressed this thought in his " Book of Hours ":

> Those who create are like unto Thee:
> They want eternity. They say: stone,
> Be eternal. And that means: be thine.

Art ranges over a wide scale: from the playful and ornamental to the most deeply moving, from childish make-believe to the loftiest confession of personal faith, from the simplest statement of a single truth to an all-encompassing world view. Reflecting every mood, it spreads before us the fullness of human experience. At the same time, by never achieving finality it points to what may still come and reminds us of Christ's promise of the more abundant life.

The response to art may have as many individual variations as that to faith. Some minds are too barren to receive either; others accept them happily, without reflection. But the deepest truths of the faith, and the real greatness of art, reveal themselves only to those who are willing to approach them with a searching, open, and teachable mind. For great art demands serious effort on our part; it discloses itself as little to the casual glance as the mystery of the faith. "The enjoyment of art does not originate in a softening or relaxing process but in intensification of all our energies," Ernst Cassirer wrote. "As soon as we fail to concentrate and give way to a mere play of pleasurable feelings and associations, we have lost sight of the work of art as such." [5]

The study of the history of art is no less exacting a mental discipline than the study of a science or of theology. But no historical interpretation alone is sufficient unless it prepares us for personal response and commitment. The work of art becomes a meaningful part of our life when we are ready to answer to it not merely intellectually but with our whole being, when it leads us to look at the world with new eyes. Each new discovery widens the scope of our love and understanding; we cannot remain the same persons we were. The opening up of personality in this experience can be a step toward the "rebirth" of which the apostle Paul so often speaks as the gateway to faith.

Nor can we overlook the element of release in our response to the work of art. Modern psychology has abundantly proved the danger for our mental health of repressed feelings. Lack of ability to express them may cause an anguish quite as acute. By making explicit what we were vainly trying to say, the work of art liberates us from the helpless agony of silence and will assume a highly personal significance for us. The poet or painter has become our spokesman; our own heartbeat pulses in the music of the composer. Any work we have truly made our own becomes an enduring friend, a cherished companion on our way, yet every time we return to it we will find new meaning and beauty in it.

 For great works of art are inexhaustible. They retain the quality of newness no matter how many minds they have enriched. The art of the past and present is a storehouse of expressed truth open to all. It invites exploration: we never know whether some work of the most vital potential value for us may not just be waiting to be discovered. The more familiar we become with this vast treasure trove, the more readily will we find help at the time of need. We may well rejoice that much-improved techniques of reproduction now make it possible for the world's great art to join in our homes the works of the composers that high-fidelity recordings are making available in outstanding performances. Christians need not fear that these masterpieces will usurp the place that belongs to the Bible. Knowing that " every good endowment and every perfect gift is from above, coming down from the Father of lights with whom there is no variation or shadow due to change " (James 1:17), we will find in the great masters of the arts forceful proof for the continuous, ongoing revelation of the spirit of God, and return from them to his Word time and again with deeper insights and love.

B. The Problem of Form

What enables art to enrich us is the principle of form. Without form there is only chaos, the indistinguishable welter of nonbeing, vaporous, elusive, meaningless. God created the universe by the act of giving form to the formless. Similarly, man's creative power, on his incomparably lesser scale, reveals itself in his ability to single out an observation or truth and, by forming it, to endow it with existence. Thoughts come and go, leaving only faint traces of their passing like atomic particles in a cloud chamber, but the thought that has crystallized into form lives on with an independent, almost indestructible, life of its own.

Pure form as such, however, is sterile. It is no more than a

decorative pattern and lends itself to endless repetition that, in
the end, becomes mechanical. A circle, for instance, though
perfect as an example of form, has little or nothing to say unless we give it content or meaning as a ring, a wheel, the outline of a face, or else use it metaphorically by speaking of the
circle of the family or of friendship. Augustine could interpret
it as a symbol of God's perfection. Yet form and expression are
not opposites, as is sometimes asserted. Unless form is expressive, it remains empty; without form, on the other hand, expression is incoherent and evaporates. To find meaningful
form in the unending stream of thoughts and sensory stimuli is
the prerogative and chief task of the creative artist. It implies
selection and condensation. "Unless there is com-pression,
nothing is ex-pressed." [6] For that reason we rarely remember
photographs we see in newspapers; a snapshot of a scene is
formless because the camera is not selective, does not leave out
unessential detail. A photograph becomes memorable when it
follows similar principles of concentration as the work of art;
when the photographer has chosen his angle, and arranged the
distribution on the scene of light and shadow, to produce a
clear pattern capable of conveying to us what he wants to
communicate.

Form thus always involves the process of "abstraction" in
the literal sense of the term, that is, withdrawing or taking
away. In his search for the secret of meaningful form the artist
must first of all learn to discriminate between the essential and
the nonessential. The beginner in art is tempted to include every observed detail in order to give a "correct" representation;
he is the slave rather than the master of the sense of sight. As
he gains experience he learns to leave out what is unnecessary
for the desired effect. He may avail himself of various methods
to emphasize vitally important parts and draw our attention to
them. Strong outlines, striking contrasts of light and shadow,
the use of exaggeration and distortion for the sake of emotional
emphasis, are a few of them. Or he may choose a close-up, almost microscopic view, as Dürer did in his admirable water-

color studies of birds' wings, small animals, or patches of grassland. These little masterpieces bring to our attention aspects of nature that might otherwise have escaped our observation entirely.

The artist of our time faces more difficult problems in his quest for adequate form than did his colleague in times past who could share in a well-established tradition and could freely borrow from others. We demand originality, and our much more comprehensive knowledge of the formal solutions of every period and civilization makes us apt to suspect plagiarism as soon as we discover similarities. This critical tendency has resulted in a frantic search for originality at any cost among many younger artists. They feel goaded toward exaggerated shock effects in the hope of being noticed in a fiercely competitive, overcommercialized art "market," where a work may be bought for financial speculation or investment instead of for aesthetic enjoyment. A given artistic style used to last for a generation, if not for a century and more, without major change. Today the most advanced fashion may dominate for a few years and be discarded in less than a decade. Artists doubt if there is enough time for the development of solid craftsmanship and the slow, gradual process of growing into maturity. Conditions beyond their control encourage them to produce too rapidly and exhibit too soon, with the unavoidable consequence of a great deal of ephemeral work. The lack of sufficient, steady patronage on the part of the churches has doubtless contributed to this hectic pace.

Yet the truly creative artist, today as always, realizes the need to pursue his way undeterred by the clamor around him. He must find his own language and forms that are right and just because what he has to say cannot be said in any other way. When a work of art convinces us, after thorough study, that not one detail could be added or left out, not one brush stroke be changed without serious impairment to the whole, we are justified in calling it a masterpiece. But if the artist himself was not fully convinced, or had not arrived at a clear understanding of his purpose, his work will unfailingly reveal weaknesses. What is shoddy, superficial, or pretentious will be unmasked as soon as the first captivating or spectacular impression wears off. Unresolved conflicts in motivation and aim also destroy the effectiveness of the message. In art as in life "no one can serve two masters."

A great work of art grows on us with prolonged contemplation because living form always reflects some aspect of the universe and thereby transcends the given reality. The painter Max Beckmann had this in mind when he said: "What I want to show in my work is the idea which hides itself behind so-called reality. I am seeking for the bridge which leads from the visible to the invisible." Vincent van Gogh wrote of his wish "to express the love of two lovers by a marriage of two complementary colors, their mingling and their opposition, the mysterious vibrations of kindred tones. To express the thought of a brow by the radiance of a light tone against a somber background. To express hope by some star, the eagerness of a soul by a sunset radiance. Certainly there is nothing in that of stereoscopic realism, but is it not something that actually exists?" [7]

Beckmann and Van Gogh were more articulate than most other artists in explaining why they had to go beyond the representation of things as they appear to the eye. Painters and sculptors generally find it difficult to put their ideas into words; if they could do so more readily, they might have become writers instead. Yet wherever artists and their friends gather, they will quickly engage in animated discussion of their thoughts. There are, happily, no final answers to the questions involved. The approaches to artistic form are as manifold as life itself. In the present age the advances of the physical and social sciences have introduced a complexity that cannot be reduced to the comparatively simple formulations of the past.

It ought not to surprise us if the arts of our time are difficult to understand — so are modern physics and the psychoanalysis of Freud and Jung. Deeply influenced in their entire outlook by the technological and scientific developments of recent

years and the almost unbelievable new sights, sounds, and
rhythms, the creative artists of today no longer believe in the
rules or laws of earlier times. These, after all, were established
before anyone had seen a neon-lighted city square or an X-ray
photograph, had crossed oceans and continents in a jet plane,
been an eyewitness in his own home of events occurring thousands of miles away, heard jazz music, or learned of nuclear
fission and missiles. The artist claims for himself the same freedom to explore the unknown and untried that the scientist and
engineer enjoy, and he is willing to accept the risks as part of
his situation. Not every rocket goes into orbit; not every venture
in the arts will prove of lasting value.

To complain of the "anarchy" of modern art is to apply
yardsticks of the past. Today's painters and sculptors are as
seriously involved in their work as were those of old, and just
as critical of their own efforts. They will not sell what does not
represent them to their satisfaction. Their constant self-criticism and urge to achieve ever more valid statements is proof of
their artistic ethos. At times they will depict the meaninglessness and the lack of faith in much of modern life; yet their
firm convictions of the values to which they aspire are a dynamic
force rooted in the same deep levels of personality from which
faith arises. Ultimately both faith and art depend on what Christians call " grace "; both affirm the world in the sense of Albert
Schweitzer's " reverence for life."

C. Beauty, Order, Truth

The values artists seek to realize are closely interrelated. To
single out one of them, even if it be the ideal of beauty, en-
dangers the unity of the work of art and leads to faulty conclusions. As John Keats assured us eloquently, beauty and truth
are one. Augustine described beauty as the splendor of order
or of truth.

There are many definitions of beauty. All agree in considering it a quality of perception involving an act of personal response, which explains why we differ in our ideas of the beauti-

ful. The individual's sense of beauty is an answer to what speaks to him at a particular stage of his growth, what evokes his love. Plotinus thought of beauty as something the soul recognizes from ancient knowledge, welcoming it and entering into unison with it. Longing for beauty was to him a longing for home, for goodness, for truth, for God.

Beauty is demanding. We react to it with our whole being, not with our senses only. It makes us painfully aware of our own imperfection, yet at the same time lifts us above ourselves in admiration, even awe. In its presence selfish desire is stilled. We want to contemplate rather than possess. We sense more deeply our kinship with all creation, and are more willing to serve.

There is a vital difference between the beautiful on the one hand and the pretty, the charming, the tasteful, the attractive or appealing, on the other. These terms describe what pleases the senses and enhances our general feeling of well-being, but remains too closely bound up with matter to affect life at its deepest. If a person permits the satisfaction of the senses to become his dominant orientation, he will turn into a shallow pleasure seeker. The early church wisely placed gluttony among the cardinal sins; aesthetic gluttony may endanger our lives as much as the culinary variety. Like wealth, power, or knowledge, beauty can assume the status of an idol. The aesthete who makes beauty his sole preoccupation shuts himself off from possibilities of growth. Fortunately, cases of such sterile worship at the altar of beauty have been rare.

Fear that beauty could distract the faithful from pure worship of God caused certain Christian churchmen of ascetic cast to reject it entirely. They suspected anything beautiful as Satan's attempt to beguile man and make him love this world more than he ought to. We wonder today how they justified their attitude in view of the many passages in the Scriptures praising lovely and delightful things and, in particular, the Song of Songs, that immortal hymn to beauty. Christ extolled the beauty of the lilies of the field, Paul admonished the Philippians: "Whatever is true, whatever is honorable, whatever is just, whatever is pure, whatever is lovely, whatever is gracious, if there is any excellence, if there is anything worthy of praise, think about these things" (Phil. 4:8). Paul knew, as did Jesus, that to the pure in heart the beauty of creation is a token and reminder of the all-surpassing beauty of God, the beauty that the psalmist longed to behold. When ascetic Christians scorned beauty they mainly succeeded in making the faith appear cold and loveless. Instead of growing in goodness and love of neighbor, they and their disciples developed a narrow-minded self-righteousness, and in their fanaticism often violated the Savior's first and greatest commandment.

Where goodness and mercy are, beauty will be also, praising God with the sound of trumpet, lute, harp, and timbrel (Ps. 150) and through forms and colors as well. Frederick Ward Kates put this thought into these words: "One of the most persuasive assurances we have of God comes through the avenue of the beautiful. A thing of beauty is the eternal in the world about us, God alive in the present; it is God speaking to us today. To watch the beautiful, to cherish it, and to seek for it, is to have begun to walk the pathway that leads to God." [8]

The beauty of a work of art can inspire us to the same deep feeling of gratitude that every sensitive mind experiences before the beauty of nature. Despite its new and different formal language, modern art can have the same effect. If we find it more difficult to accept these new forms, let us remember how long it took before the artistic beauty of Renoir's or Gauguin's masterpieces was recognized. To the Christian, all true works of art, regardless of the widest variations in style and technique, are voices in a great choir of praise.

We surely have no right to make an exception for the representation in art of the human body in its marvelous perfection, the last and greatest work to come from the hands of the Creator, who himself took on human form in the person of Jesus Christ. To despise the body as evil is a false view of the teaching of Christ and runs counter to many passages in the Scriptures. Such life-negating views originated as a reaction to the gross immorality prevalent in the Roman Empire at the time of the beginning of Christianity. Our present civilization doubtless tolerates too much laxity and open sensuality, especially in the media of mass communication. The unhealthy overemphasis on the sexual actually indicates a cynical undervaluation of the body and its functions, which deprives them of their simple dignity and degrades them to irresponsible play acting. Organic hunger is being shortchanged into mere appetite. Hunger can be satisfied, and the natural rhythms of tension and release increase well-being, but appetite remains insatiable. Moreover, its incessant stimulation is usually intended to serve commercial purposes. Ultimately, it defeats itself and leaves nothing but boredom and disgust. The equally unsound opposite extreme is an exaggerated prudery. Strong feelings of guilt and anxiety caused by the conflict between a powerful drive and the conventions of society are being "overcompensated" into a moralistic opposition against any direct and healthy artistic representation of the body.

Whenever the Scriptures approach the physical aspects of human life, they treat them with complete frankness in a serious, mature way. We find the same attitude of respect in the works of the great artists, who want to share with us their admiration of the beauty of the human body, not to incite lascivious thoughts. Neither should we be afraid to let our children see such masterpieces, provided we have taught them to think of their own bodies as "temples of the Holy Spirit" (I Cor. 6:19). The decisive question is whether the artist speaks honestly, without subterfuge, or whether his cunning arrangement betrays an intention to arouse desire. It is indeed regrettable that the church should fail to make this distinction, admittedly not always an easy one. Yet the church has not consistently rejected the representation of the undraped human body. The figures of Adam and Eve graced many churches and cathedrals from early Christian times to the eighteenth century. Paintings of the Madonna often showed her nursing the infant

Jesus at her breast, surely the most natural act of motherly love. Today some Christians will even object to seeing the Christ-child unclothed in the arms of his mother.

The house of God is the place to lead our thoughts from the visible to the invisible. It must therefore emphasize the spiritual rather than the physical. Yet they cannot be completely separated. Does not the Christian faith sanctify all life to God: soul, mind, and body? Our position should be equally distant from overemphasis on the body and from embarrassed denial or contempt, in the light of Paul's insight: "You are not your own; you were bought with a price. So glorify God in your body" (I Cor. 6:19-20).

Attempts to reduce the concept of beauty to an immutable set of proportions or to an exclusive range of subjects have proved futile. It is always changing because artists are sensitive to the thought currents of their time. Some of the most significant works of the last half century clearly reflect our greatly increased understanding of the deeper strata of personality and the lasting effect of early infancy experiences. They afford surprising new insights into the unconscious and the dream, a revelation of beauty in the casual, the commonplace, the neglected areas of life. At the same time we have gained a wholly new appreciation of the art of the child and have learned to enjoy its imaginative freedom, its spontaneous rhythms and patterns. Parents who used to laugh at the creative efforts of their children now find them charming and expressive. Not a few fathers and mothers have indeed been inspired to cast old inhibitions to the winds and try their own hands. Does this not remind us of Jesus' words: "Unless you turn and become like children, you will never enter the kingdom of heaven" (Matt. 18:3)?

Jesus' concern was for the unfeigned sincerity and trust of the child; he did not decry maturity of mind. The artist knows that the one vital element of beauty beyond the capacity of the child is order. Much of the antagonism against contemporary art is due to its apparent lack of order and clarity, causing many people to react with irritation. Yet if an "abstract" painting seems at first haphazard and chaotic, closer analysis may show a carefully considered arrangement; the painter, however, has abandoned the representation of objects to sing freely of the beauty of form and color. Rhythms, contrasts and harmonies, movements forward and backward, sudden surprises, leave ample room for the viewer's imagination and provide the fascination of a voyage of discovery. Time can be relied upon to eliminate second-rate efforts that merely follow the prevailing fashion; already, however, it is apparent that modern art has created means of formal expression that reflect the spirit of the age.

Order and form by themselves are mechanical and soulless. The most perfectly functioning machine lacks precisely the most vital quality of human life: freedom of choice. It knows neither the possibility of change (other than breakdown) nor the creative pause. Abstract art has not always avoided the pitfalls of too rigid order on the one hand, lack of organization on the other. Entirely unplanned spontaneity can easily become vacuous and, like "mood music," offer little besides entertainment. Such works may look intriguing and attractive but are scarcely more than arabesques drawn on the margins of life. The appeal of this type of art to some of our younger painters and sculptors, and to the sophisticated among the public, indicates a dangerous tendency in our civilization. Beset by fears, without a clear sense of individuality, tied up in social structures too vast to comprehend, much less to direct, modern man tries to hide his vague anxiety behind all kinds of escape mechanisms. Pacifying drugs, alcohol, escapist literature and art, are sought as means to get away from it all. We engage in useless and, indeed, pleasureless activities in order to kill time. We surround ourselves with incessant noise because we are afraid of silence and solitude, afraid of having to face ourselves.

Art is a barometer of the pressure systems of an age. The thoughtful observer notes the storm signals of a world drifting toward the catastrophe of nuclear war in some of the art of our time. Responsible artists refuse to show us a nonexisting world of undisturbed beauty, at peace with itself. They will not give a Hollywood version of life dressed up in the false hues of technicolor. They are convinced that of the values toward which art aspires, truth is the highest. Truth widens and deepens our spiritual life; untruth, be it ever so attractively dressed up, diminishes it. Every truth newly perceived through the medium of a work of art helps us to grow closer to the essence of being, to the Father of all truth.

The demand of truth may make it unavoidable to the artist to reveal the tragedy and disharmony of life. Such works can be very disconcerting until we apprehend that the genius of the artist has endowed the "ugly" with a spiritual beauty of its own. To accept it, we must free ourselves from pride and prejudice, for the bigot will never see it. If an artist shows a leper in the appalling hideousness of his disease, or if he dares to show the physical and moral corruption of society, the bigot turns away and calls for the censor. He cannot understand that Christ's commandment of love includes those least lovable, that he could touch a leper and promise the despised tax collectors and harlots the Kingdom of Heaven before the priests and elders.

These outcasts of humanity were not "ugly" to Jesus. Because he saw their intrinsic worth behind the disfigurement of sin and disease, they could face the truth about themselves and come to him to be made whole. He who drove the money-changers from the Temple of God would recognize in the bitter anguish of the socially conscious art of our time a spirit akin to his own teaching, an outcry against a society that hypocritically condemns the sinner but permits sin to flourish unmolested.

The artist's imperative need to speak the truth will express itself also in the visual forms he chooses. Violently clashing colors, sharply breaking and splintering lines, reflect his consciousness of living in a world that totters precariously on the brink of the abyss. Serious artists of our time will have nothing to do with slogans like "Take it easy" or "Keep smiling." Some feel they must call out at the top of their voices in a desperate effort to break through our callous indifference. Others speak quietly, convinced, with the existential writers and philosophers, of the absurdity of a world where man has become a stranger. The use of such apparently worthless materials as rags, pieces of wood, paper, wire, or nails in their compositions may be considered both a confession of spiritual poverty (and to discover that "is to achieve a positive conquest by the spirit") and an exaltation of some of the "humble and dirty little corners of existence" against the inhuman threat of material forces relentlessly crushing the individual.[9]

These attempts to create an almost pathetically unglamorous new beauty cannot be lightly dismissed. We recall the word of the psalmist: "The stone which the builders rejected has become the chief cornerstone" (Ps. 118:22); and Paul's great truth: "God chose what is foolish in the world to shame the wise, God chose what is weak in the world to shame the strong" (I Cor. 1:27).

Art thus probes the spiritual foundations of our civilization. As Paul Gauguin asked in a strangely beautiful and moving painting, it puts the haunting questions: Where do we come from? What are we? Where are we going? Yet here and there we can discover artists, usually little recognized by the eager followers of prevailing fashions, who dare to offer answers. They are showing us that life has the depths of guilt and sorrow, but that it also offers fulfillment, joy, and love. We can share with them the warmth of friendship, the courage expressed in selfless deeds, the soul-filling glow of true love. They remind us that the beauty of flowers, trees, animals, fields, and mountains still touches our hearts, that the eyes of children still shine with trust in the goodness of life.

In the midst of our anxieties creative artists help turn our thoughts to Him who brings tidings of peace to each one willing to listen. In contemplating their works, we find challenge and the call to action, but also rest and refreshment for our souls. Whatever outward form the artist may give to his vision, the very fact that despite everything he continues to create, even now, is an assurance of his faith in the future. Every true work of art thus points, at its deepest level of meaning, to the ultimate, to the Kingdom of God.

Chapter II

Our Heritage

He who can read the style of a culture can discover its ultimate concern, its religious substance.

— Paul Tillich.

A. The Background

The Christian churches are not yet of one mind regarding the place of the arts in the service of God. Some welcome them with open arms; others remain suspicious, if not outright hostile. Opposition to the use of painting and sculpture has become so closely identified with the Protestant Reformation that it is widely understood as one of the major differences between Protestantism and Roman Catholicism and accepted without further thought. Yet the Reformation was not the first movement in the history of the Christian faith to turn against the arts, and Protestants have not arrived at general agreement.

The problem is much older. It dates back to the struggle of the Israelites to rise above the idol worship of their neighbors. When they left the intellectual and emotional blind alley of polytheism, the " chosen people " came to understand that no image made by human hands can conceivably encompass the reality of the one God, Creator and Ruler of the universe. This insight crystallized in the Second Commandment: " You shall not make yourself a graven image, or any likeness of anything that is in heaven above, or that is in the earth beneath, or that is in the water under the earth; you shall not bow down to them or serve them " (Ex. 20:4-5).

It was a truly revolutionary law, for since the dawn of history man had felt the urge to visualize his gods. Every primitive civilization has produced such images, from crude clay idols to intricately wrought figures in stone or metal. The overwhelming powers of nature and, at a later stage, abstract ideas of law and order became concrete and "real" in them. Man's need to propitiate the gods could be satisfied by ritual offerings and ministrations to the images. Gradually a priestly caste evolved to administer the more and more exacting ceremonies. Closeness to the revered image gave the priest his high standing, often including power over life and death.

By and large, the Jewish people adhered to the law against image worship. We know of no representations of the God of the Bible. Yet the Biblical books themselves, and archaeological evidence, prove that the Jews were too intimately linked with the nations around them not to be affected by their way of thinking. Figures of the goddess Astarte have been unearthed in Palestine, and recent excavations in the ancient city of Hazor disclosed the existence there of a small Israelite settlement where an idolatrous cult flourished. Persistent tendencies to idolatry called forth the prophets' most emphatic warnings. They used reason, irony, and threats to cure the people of their folly. Idol worship was held responsible for the defeats the nation suffered. Deuteronomy forbids the making and worshiping of idols under penalty of death.

The Old Testament, however, leaves no doubt that the Second Commandment was directed against the idolatrous worship of images rather than against the visual arts as such. The detailed instructions for the building of the Ark of the Covenant provide for two cherubim of gold to overshadow the mercy seat with their wings, symbolic figures whose origin lies in the Babylonian-Assyrian-Hittite civilizations. Cherubim were also used, as were palm trees, flowers, and pomegranates, to decorate Solomon's Temple. We hear of the molten sea, a large bronze basin supported by twelve bronze bulls, of elaborately shaped lampstands, and of the ornate throne of Solo-

mon. All of this presupposes a flourishing tradition of craftsmanship among the Jews.

Under the impact of the Hellenistic civilization the Jews
adopted a more lenient interpretation of the Mosaic law against
images. Jewish coins from the Maccabees to Bar-Cochba show
various plants, architectural details, and musical instruments.
Those made for the Herodias family bear portrait heads of the
rulers in the manner of Roman coins of the time. Ornamental
carvings in stone adorned the synagogues of Capernaum and
other localities, and mosaic floors were frequently laid out with
similar designs. The most significant find of recent years was
made during the excavation of the caravan city of Dura-
Europos on the Euphrates, destroyed in A.D. 256. In a house
used as a synagogue, nearly sixty wall paintings with stories
from the Bible were discovered. They are too advanced in style
and technique to have been the independent work of a local
artist, and make it necessary to assume the existence of earlier
models, or perhaps of illustrated Septuagint manuscripts made
for the Hellenized Jews in such large centers of population as
Alexandria. Since none of these has as yet come to light, the
Dura-Europos murals, now in the Damascus museum, remain
the oldest Jewish Bible illustrations known.[1]

It was a short-lived development. The Second Commandment had become too firmly established among the Jews, now
widely scattered in the Diaspora, to permit the growth of an indigenous art, except on a minor scale. Their creative energies
turned to other fields until, after the emancipation in the nineteenth century, a number of Jewish painters and sculptors rose
to prominence. Some of them, foremost, Marc Chagall, have
been deeply inspired by the Bible. In recent years modern
American synagogues have made impressive use of abstract or
near-abstract art forms.

B. Early Christian Times

The Christian faith grew up on the foundation of the Old
Testament and took over the commandment against idolatry.

It became one of the chief distinctions between the early congregations and the pagan cults flourishing in the Roman Empire. Faith in God as spirit and belief in his invisible nature
made the worship of images "resembling mortal man or birds
or animals or reptiles" (Rom. 1:23) appear foolish indeed.
This spirituality attracted numerous converts from among
thoughtful men and women who were repelled by the popular
imageries then in vogue. The presence of many Jewish Christians also tended to inhibit figurative art. When the congregations had become sufficiently organized to require larger places
of assembly and worship, the persecutions set in and prevented
the building of churches. Besides, the books of the New Testament, the chief source for later Christian art, did not become
available in their entirety until the middle of the second century. Also, as long as the church lived in constant expectation
of the Second Coming of Christ and the end of the age, artistic
efforts must have appeared futile.

It is thus not surprising that few if any surviving examples
of Christian art can safely be dated before the third century.
From that time on they are found in increasing numbers in the
Christian communities of Italy, Asia Minor, and Egypt. Early
Christian art is predominantly sepulchral art, designed to honor
the memory of the dead and to strengthen the living in their
faith in eternal life and salvation. We meet it on the sculptured sarcophagi that wealthier members of the congregations
commissioned for their burial in accordance with Roman custom, on gold glasses, lamps, ivory carvings, and in the paintings of the catacombs.

The dark passages and chambers of the catacombs witnessed
the first outpouring of Christian piety in visual form. By the
flickering light of oil lamps pious hands adorned the walls and
ceilings of these subterranean burial places outside Rome,
Naples, Syracuse, and other large cities with scenes from the
Scriptures, symbols, and signs. They used the quick, expressive
style current in Rome and familiar to us from the wall paintings
of Pompeii. The best-liked subjects were graphic reminders of

God's power to save: Moses striking water from the rock for
the thirsting multitude, Jonah saved from the belly of the fish,
Daniel unharmed in the lions' den, the three youth miraculously preserved in the fiery furnace, Isaac spared at the last
moment. In the light of the new revelation these scenes assumed even greater significance: the water pouring from the
rock could suggest the water of baptism (cf. I Cor. 10:1-4);
the story of Jonah; the resurrection (Matt. 12:40). The precise
instant of the incarnation was indicated in the annunciation
scene; the adoration of the Magi meant the revelation of Christ
to the Gentiles. We also find representations of Christ's baptism in the River Jordan, the raising of Lazarus, the healing of
the paralytic and of the woman with the issue of blood, the
multiplication of loaves and fishes, and the wedding at Cana.
The paintings are not storytelling in the full sense of the word.
Their formulalike shortness expresses in symbolic form the
central idea of the faith: the certainty of salvation for the
"remnant chosen by grace" (Rom. 11:5). They were not intended as works of art but as visual reassurance, by means of
historical proof, of the validity of the faith.

Any sensitive visitor walking through the long, narrow cor-
ridors past the rectangular or semicircular openings in the
walls for the bodies of the dead, and the often touchingly naïve
decorations faintly preserved here and there, will be deeply
stirred. Simple inscriptions on the graves — " In pace," " Vivas
in Christo " — remind us poignantly of the confessors who once
sought refuge here in times of danger, and who at last were
laid to rest among friends, in the full certainty of their glorious
resurrection. Their steadfast courage kept the faith alive in the
days of its gravest peril and preserved it for us.

In times of severe persecution the language of the symbol
was the only possible means of communication. When the early
Christians dared not openly pronounce the name of the Savior,
they could still confess their allegiance to him by the sign of
the fish. The Greek word ichthus provided an acrostic formed
by the initials of the greeting, " Jesus Christ, Son of God,

Savior." It also suggested the water of baptism and, through reference to the miracle of the loaves and fishes, the Eucharist. These connotations made the fish the most frequently used symbol for Christ. It is often accompanied by the anchor, symbol of hope, whose horizontal bar made it also a reminder of the cross, and by the letters Alpha and Omega, the first and last of the Greek alphabet quoted in The Revelation to John (ch. 1:8) to describe the all-embracing majesty of the Lord.

There is no evidence whatever that the early Christians made carvings, paintings, or symbols into objects of worship. The Protestant Reformers might have thought more highly of Christian art had the catacombs not been rediscovered in 1578 but a century earlier. Yet already at the turn of the third century some warning voices were heard against the use of the visual arts. Clement of Alexandria, Tertullian, and Origen reminded their fellow believers of the strict letter of the Mosaic law. They were anxious to keep the church untainted by any suspicion of the idolatry still rampant among non-Christians. Their opposition to images was the more outspoken because the first Christian artists could not invent an entirely new pictorial language but borrowed freely from late classical art, though they filled the adopted forms with a new meaning. Many symbolic figures of early Christian art originated in Greek or Roman concepts. Christ could be seen as Orpheus, for instance, because his gentle voice would bring even the most hardened sinners to reason just as Orpheus quieted the wild animals when he sang to them. Among the decorations of the catacombs, and on a number of sarcophagi, we find the same little genii who playfully re-enact the occupations of grownups on Pompeiian frescoes. They climb cheerfully through the vines on the vault mosaics of the church of Sta. Constanza in Rome, where they gather grapes and trample them in symbolic reference to the Eucharist. The peacock, in classical antiquity a symbol of immortality, since his flesh was believed to remain unspoiled after death, could now symbolize Christ's resurrection. Even the favorite figure of the Good Shepherd carrying a lamb on his shoulder owes its origin to the Greek statue of Hermes Criophoros, the ram bearer. (PLATE 1)

Other images were suggested by the New Testament. As all four Gospels identify the dove that descended on Christ's head after his baptism with the Holy Spirit, it has always signified the third Person of the Trinity. John the Baptist's words, "Behold, the Lamb of God, who takes away the sin of the world!" (John 1:29), Paul's mention of Christ as our "paschal lamb" (I Cor. 5:7), and the apocalyptic vision of Rev., ch. 14, made the lamb a readily understood symbol of the Savior. Isaiah's prophecy of the Suffering Servant who, like a lamb, is led to the slaughter (Isa. 53:7) and a similar passage in Jeremiah (ch. 11:19) lent further weight to the symbol. Often the lamb is seen standing on the rock of the faith from which the four rivers of Paradise flow, indicating the four Gospels and their origin in Christ.

Considerable time elapsed before early Christian art solved its most difficult problem, the representation of the Savior himself. There is no authentic portrait of Christ, that is, one made from life. We know of no artist in the Palestine of his day who could have made one. The Jewish people frowned on portraiture, and had Jesus permitted such a violation of the law, his enemies would have used it as a potent weapon against him. The legend of Luke's painting a portrait of Mary did not arise until the fifth century, probably through the literal interpretation of a figure of speech. For it was often remarked that his Gospel gives a more complete "portrait" of Christ's mother than do any of the other Gospels. It was natural that he should later become the patron saint of painters. Flemish artists of the fifteenth century frequently show him busy at his easel making a portrait study of the Madonna and her child, but there is no historical evidence whatever for it.

We hear of a statue of Christ being in the possession of Emperor Alexander Severus, who is also said to have owned statues of Abraham, Orpheus, and other "particularly holy spirits," but the reference (in the *Historia Augusta* of Aelius

Lampridius) does not imply an authentic portrait.[2] Nor can
the Turin shroud, on which some claim to see the imprint of
Christ's features, or the *Holy Face,* a painting preserved in
the cathedral of Lucca, Italy, be seriously considered contemporary with Christ.

The New Testament gives not a single description of Jesus'
physical appearance. At best, it offers a few indirect hints.
The Samaritan woman immediately recognized him as a Jew,
but whether by his clothing or his looks we cannot tell. Had
his stature been in any way conspicuous, Judas would not
have needed to single him out from among the disciples with
a kiss; nor would the two followers have failed to recognize
him on the road to Emmaus. These inconclusive suggestions
accord with Paul's word about Jesus' having taken "the form
of a servant, being born in the likeness of men" (Phil. 2:7).

After the last eyewitnesses had died and the church had
spread far and wide in a Gentile world thoroughly accustomed to portraiture, the desire for a representation of the
founder of the faith became irresistible. We hear of the request for such a portrait addressed by Constantia, sister of
Emperor Constantine, to the learned Bishop Eusebius of
Caesarea, who was strongly opposed to anything reminiscent
of idolatry and who tried to convince her of her error. How
could any human hand attempt to create an adequate image
of Christ when even his own disciples on Mt. Tabor could not
endure the radiance of his divine grace, and when Paul could
speak of the "glory of God in the face of Christ" (II Cor.
4:6)?

Other churchmen were less adamant. They pointed out that
Christ had assumed human form and had suffered pain and
death as does any other human being. As long as images did
not receive idolatrous veneration, the portrayal of Jesus the
man could therefore not violate the law. This view prevailed
after the victory of the church under Constantine, and was
further strengthened by the need to counteract heretical doctrines of the nature of Christ. To deny the right to represent

him might encourage those who had cast doubt on the reality of his human existence.

In its efforts to solve the problem, early Christian art developed two distinct types of representation, both intended as symbolical rather than as actual portraits. For several centuries they occur side by side, sometimes on the same sarcophagus or in the same church. One shows him as youthful, almost boyish, reminiscent of the classic Apollo. The beauty of his regular features suggests the timeless being of the divine Logos. We find Christ thus portrayed on numerous sarcophagi, among them that of Junius Bassus, a Roman official who died in 358. The large work, a masterpiece of sculpture preserved in the crypt of St. Peter's in Rome, presents Christ three times: riding into Jerusalem, taken prisoner, and seated in glory between Peter and Paul. In the latter scene Caelus, god of the sky, appears under Christ's throne holding up the canopy of heaven, a characteristic example of the use of pagan concepts that had lost their cult implications and could no longer offend Christian sensibilities. By the same token, personifications of places and rivers typical of late classic art occur in Christian works of this period and survive into later times with no more implied meaning than to identify a given locality. The boyish figure of Christ also entered the great apsidal mosaics of some early churches (San Aquilino, Milan; San Vitale, Ravenna) and is seen in the lovely ivory carvings of the lipsanotheca, a decorated box preserved in Brescia, Italy.

The other type shows a considerably older, bearded Christ. It originated probably in the Near East and was modeled after the wandering Cynic philosophers, friends of the poor, whose homely appearance was a familiar sight in the cities of the Roman world. Gradually this image gained in dignity until it achieved true grandeur in imposing works of Christian art such as the large sarcophagus from the end of the fourth century in San Ambrogio, Milan. (PLATE 2)

Nobility and spiritual depth shine from the face of this Christ who stands on the rock and charges his apostles to go and preach the gospel to every nation. Despite the ravages of time, it remains one of the most inspiring representations of the Savior in art. On the reverse side of the sarcophagus he is seen once more with the apostles, this time seated, and here the youthful Christ is teaching from the book he holds in his hand. The open city gates in the background evoke the vision of the heavenly Jerusalem through whose gates, never shut by day, shall enter those "who are written in the Lamb's book of life" (Rev. 21:27). The small figures of the deceased couple for whom the sarcophagus was made kneel before the lamb in supplication. The narrow sides, and the lid, show other scenes related to the message of salvation. It is possible that the learned Ambrose, the Bishop of Milan honored by posterity as one of the four greatest Latin fathers of the church, himself devised the meaningful theological program of the impressive and beautiful work.

Other outstanding representations of the bearded Christ are preserved in the apse mosaics of SS. Cosmas and Damianus and of Sta. Pudenziana in Rome, the latter one of the oldest places of Christian worship in the city. It was built around 385 on the site of a "house church" of the first century. The mosaic interprets the text of Rev., chs. 21 and 22, by showing Christ enthroned in front of a colonnade that discloses the buildings of the New Jerusalem. (The artist apparently had in mind the famous churches built by Constantine to commemorate the Easter events.) A tall, jeweled cross rises from the hill of Calvary against a reddish-blue ground. To its sides appear the winged symbols of the four Evangelists: the man (or angel) of Matthew, the lion of Mark, the ox of Luke, and the eagle of John. They are first mentioned in a vision of the prophet Ezekiel (Ezek. 10:14) and occur again in Rev. 4:6-8, where they surround the throne and sing praises to God.

Led by Paul (on Christ's right) and Peter (on his left), the disciples look up to the Master to receive his command. Two women behind them represent the Church of the Circumcision and the Church of the Gentiles — the Old and New Testaments. A frieze at the bottom showed the faithful, symbolized as usual by sheep, approaching the Lamb of God on the hill with the "river of the water of life" flowing from it. This frieze was removed in the course of later restorations, much to the detriment of the entire composition and its message.

Still, enough remains of this awe-inspiring vision of the Parousia, the eternal reign of Christ, to call the visitor to meditation on the last things: death and resurrection, judgment and salvation. The unknown artist stressed the abstract design elements and refrained from making figures and background realistic. Several apostles on the right, restored in an entirely realistic style, clearly demonstrate the superiority of the older work; they look like actors on a stage and do not communicate the transcendental feeling that is alive in the untouched figures.

When the church emerged from the darkness of the persecution era and began to build large houses of worship, two major tendencies developed. The West preferred the so-called basilican plan which was adapted, perhaps through the influence of early Jewish synagogues, from the Roman market hall or basilica. It provides for a long nave, from the Latin word *navis*, ship, symbolizing the task of the church to carry the faithful to heaven as a ship carries men across the seas to a safe harbor. The nave ends in a semicircular apse, with the altar, usually raised by means of a few steps, as the focal point. The nave is separated from the much lower and narrower aisles on both sides by rows of columns, not infrequently taken from demolished pagan temples. Windows in the clerestory above the roofs of the aisles admit light. The stern, functional simplicity of the early churches creates an indelible impression of dignity and worshipful silence, an impression that is further deepened where old mosaics have survived.

The contribution of the East was the centralized church surmounted by one or more domes. Its greatest monument, although it incorporates some features of the longitudinal plan, is the church of Hagia Sophia, or Holy Wisdom, in Constantinople (Istanbul). The tremendous structure was built between 532 and 537 by order of Emperor Justinian. Resplendent with mosaics, silver and marble incrustation, and flooded with light from many windows at the base of the dome and in the side walls, it provided a grandiose setting for the ceremonial entry of the emperor and the colorful ritual of the Eastern church. Byzantine architecture continued to use the centralized plan, though it remained exceptional in the West, where it is best represented by San Vitale in Ravenna, Charlemagne's palace chapel at Aachen (now the center part of the cathedral), and St. Mark's in Venice.

San Vitale is only one of many jewels preserved in the small city of Ravenna to the south of Venice. Having served as a royal residence during the fifth and sixth centuries, Ravenna sank into obscurity and was bypassed by wars and invasions. Thus its glorious monuments escaped destruction and have come down to our days virtually unspoiled. The churches and baptisteries of the city, with their incomparably beautiful mosaic decoration, offer the visitor an unforgettable experience of early Christian faith and art.

There is much to admire: the little mausoleum of Galla Placidia, where luminous colors glow in the mystic light that falls through amber windowpanes of alabaster, and where the Good Shepherd feeds the faithful, offering rest and salvation for their souls; the imposing groups of Emperor Justinian and Empress Theodora, with their retinue in San Vitale; the wide nave of San Apollinare in Classe, with its columns marching in stately rhythm to the apse where radiant symbols proclaim the transfiguration of Christ. Among Ravenna's riches is the oldest surviving series of scenes from the ministry and Passion of the Lord. The clear-cut designs of these mosaic panels, high above the clerestory windows of San Apollinare Nuovo, go straight to the heart of each story and tell it reverently, without unnecessary detail. The miracle scenes have been called "visual prayers"; the Christian looking at them would perceive "a reality not past, but mysteriously present and related to his own life."

The two mosaic friezes below the windows in the same church must rank with the greatest masterpieces of art. On bright green against a golden background, long rows of saints and martyrs advance in slow procession toward the altar. The men are dressed in white tunics, the women wear golden robes over white. Blue and red accents enliven the color scheme, which evokes a festive, worshipful mood. "As the liturgy is celebrated, the basilica becomes the heavenly Jerusalem and the living congregation joins the heavenly hosts in adoration of the Lamb." [3]

The art of the early church gives expression to a joyful, even jubilant faith. It is the art of a spiritual community convinced beyond a shadow of a doubt that it has been granted the revelation of ultimate truth, and eager to proclaim it to the blessing of all mankind. In the knowledge of the love of God manifested in Jesus Christ, it looks forward to eternal life without despising God's created world. Pure in heart, it can show the beauty of human beings just as it can extol the beauty of nature in trees, flowers, and animals. It speaks of love, not of hatred; heaven rather than hell is its foremost concern. Instead of threatening punishment, it holds out the promise of greater joy to come.

Early Christian art does not give way, either, to a spirit of revenge against the enemies of the faith who had persecuted the believers. No representations of martyrdoms have come down to us. Some writers of the time mention them, but perhaps they were of the character of the St. Lawrence mosaic in the mausoleum of Galla Placidia. Here the saint stands near the iron grid on which he died, but the artist does not show his agony. Cross and open book in his hands mark him as a witness for Christ; the four Gospels on the shelves of a bookcase point to the truths for which he gave his life. In quiet confidence the mosaic seems to echo Paul's exultant words:

> O death, where is thy victory?
> O death, where is thy sting?
> (I Cor. 15:55.)

This emphasis on witness rather than on suffering may have been one of the reasons why early Christian art showed neither the crucifixion nor the deposition and entombment of Christ. It was not afraid to "preach Jesus Christ crucified," but judged the cross itself to be meaningful enough to proclaim "Christ the power of God and the wisdom of God" (I Cor. 1:24). Death was a passing moment, a doorway to an infinitely greater life. To hold it constantly before our eyes would tend to contradict Paul's testimony: "I consider that the sufferings of this present time are not worth comparing with the glory that is to be revealed to us" (Rom. 8:18).

The early church was candid enough to know its failures and weaknesses. The memory of Peter's denial of the Lord was a warning against overconfidence and false pride; the frequent representations of the scene were doubtless intended as reminders of the constant need for penitence. Judging by its surviving monuments, we can assert that early Christian art reflects the ethos of Paul's letters, in particular that to the Romans. It echoes his awareness of justification by God's "grace as a gift, through the redemption which is in Christ Jesus" (Rom. 3:24); it heeds Paul's warning against fear and vengefulness. The lack of individualization in the figures of apostles and saints suggests his word that "we, though many, are one body in Christ" (Rom. 12:5), and the pervading sense of fresh, ardent enthusiasm reminds us of his great insight that "all of us who have been baptized into Christ Jesus were baptized into his death . . . so that as Christ was raised from the dead by the glory of the Father, we too might walk in newness of life" (Rom. 6:3-5).

This is the spirit that the Protestant Reformers, led by Martin Luther, sought to recapture and revive. The art of the early church is closer to the heart of the Protestant message than is the art of any other period in so far as it refers to the community of faith; in the area of personal devotion Rembrandt remains unsurpassed. It is an encouraging sign that the most vital and expressive religious art of our time relates itself once again to this spirituality without following it in lifeless imitation. Since this is true of the best Protestant and Roman Catholic art alike, may we not hope that an increasing awareness of their common origin will, in the end, help bring the tragically divided Christian churches closer to each other?

C. The Byzantine Era

The persecutions had produced a tightly knit, dedicated Christian community. After Christianity had triumphed and become the official religion of the state, the initial fervor was bound to recede. The fall of the Roman Empire ushered in a period of political and social chaos. Harassed individuals sought consolation and support. Some withdrew from the world into the rapidly growing monasteries where the life-affirming joy of the early church paled into life-denying asceticism, exemplified by the self-tortures of the column sitters, or stylites. Others tried to find identification with the martyrs in Christ by venerating their relics and the places hallowed by their memory, and gave credence to the most fantastic legendary miracle stories. More and more complex doctrines overlaid the original kerygma and subjected the believers to the guidance of the church, which alone knew how to interpret them. The electrifying hope for the Parousia yielded to a minutely regulated, highly formalized ritual patterned after the court ceremonial of imperial Byzantium (Constantinople). These conditions offered a fertile breeding ground for the spread of superstitions and image worship among the masses. Images multiplied and were honored with prostrations, incense, and candles; they were washed, anointed, kissed. They were believed to be able to heal diseases, aid in childbearing, conquer demons, or return runaway slaves. Even the water used in washing the image might effect cures.

All of this remained on the popular level. The leading theologians either opposed the pictorial arts or, like Jerome and Augustine, accepted them with definite reservations. Yet when Bishop Serenus of Marseilles removed the images from the churches of his diocese, Pope Gregory the Great (590–604), traditionally credited with the introduction of Gregorian chant into church music, advised him that representations of religious history are well suited for purposes of instruction. They are to be used so that " those uneducated in the art of reading can, by looking at the walls, read what they are unable to read in books."

Pope Gregory's authority prevailed in the West, where the storytelling character of religious art had generally stressed the incident rather than the person. The East, particularly Syria, preferred static images that lent themselves more readily for a veneration often dangerously close to image worship. After even the "heathen" Moslems had scoffed at Christian use of imagery, the forces of opposition in the Eastern church gathered strength and finally influenced Emperor Leo III to order the removal of all images of saints, martyrs, and angels from the churches (726). His successor followed up by decreeing their destruction. The move was supported by the army and part of the episcopate, but was violently opposed by the monasteries and large sections of the populace. The ensuing iconoclastic controversy lasted over a century and was fought on both sides with the bitterness of religious fanaticism. In the end, the iconoclasts had to concede defeat, and Empress Theodora in 842–843 restored the use of images. The Greek Orthodox Church still celebrates the Sunday of Orthodoxy as a feast day in memory of the event.

The principles formulated at the Council of Nicaea in 787 remain valid for the Orthodox and the Roman Catholic Churches: "We ordain . . . that like the sign of the venerable and life-giving cross, so likewise the pious and sacred images . . . be represented, namely, the image of our Lord and

Savior Jesus Christ, of the holy mother of God, the holy angels
and of all holy and saintly men. The more frequently they are
seen, the more the observer will be reminded of the prototypes
and moved to imitate them, and to render them salutation and
homage, though not adoration, for that must only be given to
God. . . . The honor shown to the image reflects honor to the
prototype. Whoever venerates an image venerates the person
represented."

The defenders of religious art explained their convictions
with great learning. They pointed out that sight as man's foremost sense needs to be hallowed by the contemplation of the
sacred. As God had in Christ become flesh and revealed himself to man, artists were justified in making likenesses of the
Savior. To claim that Christ could not be represented would
be to deny the incarnation and with it Christ's human nature;
it would perpetuate heresies such as docetism and monophy-
sitism, which the church had long since condemned. Indeed, it
would amount to a denial of Christ's full reality, for " whatever
is entirely real must be able to become image, and thereby
prove its full reality." [4]

The religious concepts of the Greek theologians found visual
expression in the icon, literally, " image," the most characteristic art form of the Eastern churches. The icon is usually an un-
framed panel of small size intended as an aid to contemplative
worship. In the home it became the center of individual and
family devotion. Numerous icons are hung side by side to
adorn the iconostasis, or picture wall, which in the orthodox
churches separates the space assigned to the congregation
from the altar space, to which only the priest and his assistants
have access.

The painting of icons was considered a liturgical act for
which the painter prepared himself through prayerful meditation. The deeper his faith, the more convincing would be his
work. He had to stand back as a maker and let the spiritual
message take precedence, and usually he did not sign his name
to the work. Nor was he worried about artistic originality. On

the contrary, his task was to repeat, to the best of his ability, a design that had come down through centuries of faithful copying from some famous image to which tradition assigned either authenticity or a miraculous origin. The wholly spiritual intent of the icon could not be served by a naturalistic style attempting to give the illusion of three-dimensional quality, depth of space, or the light effects of the visible world. Icon painting thus continued in small scale the flat, near-abstract designs developed in the mosaics of the fifth and sixth centuries. It uses a great deal of gold to suggest the radiance of otherworldly glory, and places its figures preferably in frontal position so as to make them speak more directly to the viewer. The absence of any show of emotion, on the other hand, emphasizes the distance between him and the sacred. Quiet, inscrutable faces with eyes whose steady gaze seems to be directed into another world speak of an eternity of faith where time and change have lost all significance.

This intensely spiritual style spread from Greece and Byzantium into every Christian country, continued unbroken in the Balkan nations, and flourished in Russia into the early nineteenth century. It reached its culmination in the work of Andrev Rublev (ca. 1370–1420). From the thirteenth century on, the "sweet new style" of the Gothic superseded it in the West. When the new realism of the Renaissance came in, western Europe turned its back entirely on Byzantine art, considering it stiff and archaic. Only lately have we begun once again to understand its beauty and spiritual vigor.

The prominent place of the icon in Byzantine art must not make us overlook the great creative efforts of this period in mosaics, book illuminations, ivory carvings, enamels, and sumptuous textiles. Costly objects of small size, produced by the superbly skilled craftsmen of Byzantium, were shipped abroad and became the envied possession of the powerful and the wealthy, or found their way into the treasure rooms of cathedrals and abbey churches. Throughout the later Middle Ages they served as models for the artists of Europe as far west

as Ireland. But they also raise a thorny question that has
plagued Christian consciences ever since. Is it right for the
church of Christ to own and use objects of great material
value? Does not their very costliness encourage the sins of
pride, vanity, covetousness, and envy? Who knows how many
lives have been lost defending such treasures against invaders
attracted by gold and precious stones? Time and again the
church has had to remind itself of Jesus' warning: "Do not lay
up for yourselves treasures on earth, where moth and rust con-
sume and where thieves break in and steal, but lay up for
yourselves treasures in heaven. . . . For where your treasure
is, there will your heart be also" (Matt. 6:19-21). Concerned
Christians have often pointed to the Master's poverty, and to
his admonition to the rich young man to sell all he had and
give it to the poor.

Yet the church counters with weighty arguments. It is a
universal trait of human nature to give what we hold most
dear as an expression of love. Had not God himself, according
to the Bible, asked an offering of "gold, silver, and bronze,
blue and purple and scarlet stuff and fine twined linen . . . oil
for the lamps, spices for the anointing oil and for the fragrant
incense, onyx stones, and stones for setting, for the ephod and
for the breastpiece"? (Ex. 25:4, 6-7). Through Moses, God
had commanded rich furnishings for the Tabernacle, and garments of great splendor for Aaron, the high priest. The people
had willingly brought their "brooches and earrings and signet
rings and armlets, all sorts of gold objects, every man dedicat-
ing an offering of gold to the Lord" (Ex. 35:22). Again, later,
the leaders of the people came forth with their offerings of
beautiful and costly things, carefully listed in Num. 7:10-88.

Solomon's Temple was likewise adorned with much gold,
and when the work was finished the king brought in "the
things which David his father had dedicated, the silver, the
gold, and the vessels, and stored them in the treasuries of
the house of the Lord" (I Kings 7:51). Of other Scriptural
references the most disarming is the story of the woman who

anointed Jesus. When the disciples complained about "waste," Jesus defended her gracious action: "Let her alone; why do you trouble her? She has done a beautiful thing to me" (Mark 14:6). Many offerings of great material value have since been brought to the altar, where the Lord's death is remembered at every mass or Communion service. If sometimes the avowed intention was one of atonement, the church could not refuse the gift without forgetting how Jesus himself had been moved by the woman's act of love to declare her sins forgiven.

The debate is likely to continue as long as Christians can sincerely disagree on how best to serve God. It has extended to every visible manifestation of the faith, from the house of worship itself to vestments and hymnals. Both the starkly simple Quaker meetinghouse and the ornate Byzantine church can claim Scriptural authority, the improvised gospel tent as well as the elaborately decorated high altar of a cathedral. All may become places where the Holy Spirit acts to transform the lives of men and women. Members of the liturgical churches could learn, through personal experience, how an inspired message and a prayerful congregation can make the most modest room a shrine of the living God. Free-church Protestants would benefit from an open-minded understanding of the spiritual uplift that can come to us from a truly beautiful building dedicated to the worship of God. They need not renounce their convictions, yet would come to understand one another better. The essential condition is that God alone be worshiped, without pride or vanity, and that forms, signs, symbols, setting, and ritual do not hide him from our hearts.

Whatever one's personal views about the role of art in the Christian church, it is hard to imagine an open-minded visitor who would not be deeply impressed by the great Byzantine mosaics in Constantinople, Salonica, Daphni, Palermo, Cefalu, or Monreale. The cathedral of Monreale, built around 1200 in the hills above Palermo, Sicily, as the palace church of the Norman rulers, preserves the most complete series of Byzantine mosaics. From the capitals of the columns upward, the

walls are dressed in gold with strong blues, reds, greens, and
whites shining from this ground. Thanks to the wide interior
space of the cathedral, the splendor does not become oppres-
sive. The eye, moreover, is immediately drawn to the imposing
half-figure of the Savior on the vault of the apse. (PLATE 3)

He is the "Pantocrator," or Ruler of the All. Austere, immutable, he raises his right hand in blessing while holding the
Scriptures in his left, open to the passage: "I am the light of
the world; he who follows me will not walk in darkness, but
will have the light of life" (John 8:12). With variations, this
figure occurs in domes or apses of most Byzantine churches.
Christ's expression is sterner at Daphni, more serene at Cefalu,
but there is never the least trace of sentimentality. The concept
of the Pantocrator, and the entire decorative scheme of the
cathedral, are clearly related to the high Christology of The
Letter to the Hebrews, where Christ is called the high priest,
holy, blameless, unstained, exalted above the heavens. The
consciously simplified linear design, the majestic proportions
and the shimmering colors of the mosaic, translate into convincing visual forms the text: "He reflects the glory of God
and bears the very stamp of his nature, upholding the universe
by his word of power. . . . He sat down at the right hand of
the Majesty on high, having become as much superior to angels
as the name he has obtained is more excellent than theirs"
(Heb. 1:3-4). Colorful figures of seraphim and cherubim appear below the Pantocrator as if to illustrate this very passage.
The whole composition is imbued with the spirit of the great
affirmation: "Jesus Christ is the same yesterday and today and
forever" (Heb. 13:8). (PLATE 4)

The Biblical scenes on the walls of Monreale cathedral are
chapters in the story of salvation "declared at first by the
Lord, and it was attested to us by those who heard him, while
God also bore witness by signs and wonders and various miracles and by gifts of the Holy Spirit distributed according to
his own will" (Heb. 2:3-4). When the mosaics show the
temptation of Christ on three separate panels they underline

the words: "For we have not a high priest who is unable to sympathize with our weaknesses, but one who in every respect has been tempted as we are, yet without sinning. Let us then with confidence draw near to the throne of grace, that we may receive mercy and find grace to help in time of need" (Heb. 4:15-16).

The Ark of the Covenant "covered on all sides with gold" (Heb. 9:4) seems to be repeated in the gold-encrusted interior of Monreale. Most of the Old Testament incidents mentioned in Hebrews are also represented in the mosaics. The whole cathedral, with its many figures of saints and prophets, creates the mood of firm assurance expressed in the passage: "Therefore, since we are surrounded by so great a cloud of witnesses, let us also lay aside every weight, and sin which clings so closely, . . . looking to Jesus the pioneer and perfecter of our faith" (Heb. 12:1-2).

That the ideas of The Letter to the Hebrews were close to the thinking of the Byzantine church and influenced its art is in keeping with evidence indicating that Eastern theologians upheld the Pauline authorship of the book against doubts raised by the West. The authority of the Greek church won out in the end, and The Letter to the Hebrews was admitted to the canon of Scripture. In 1156, the Council of Constantinople strongly reaffirmed the concept of Christ as high priest, and in later Byzantine art we find images portraying him in episcopal robes.

A parallel to the high Christology of the Byzantine era is the exalted position now accorded to the Virgin Mary. Her veneration increased rapidly after the Council of Ephesus in 435 had declared her Theotokos, "Mother of God." Several clearly established variants show her holding the infant Savior on her knees or arm; he is mature beyond his years and extends his hand in benediction. The Byzantine Madonna is a figure of majesty, the "temple of the incarnate Word, the throne of God." [5] In the decorative scheme of the churches she is generally placed below the Pantocrator, though from the sixth century on she may take over the center of the apse, most impressively in the basilica of Torcello near Venice. (PLATE 5)

The faithful were eager to know more about Mary than the Gospels tell. Apocryphal writings such as the Protevangelium, or Book of James, attempted to fill the gap. Known since the second century, its popularity made it the source for countless works of art in the Middle Ages. Here we learn of Mary's parents, Joachim and Anne, of her immaculate conception, her presentation in the Temple, her betrothal to Joseph, and of the Nativity of Christ in a cave where Mary had taken shelter, with two midwives assisting her.

The so-called Gospels of Thomas and of Pseudo-Matthew add other incidents to the story of Jesus' infancy. The apocryphal account of Mary's assumption into heaven assumed great significance for doctrine as well as for art. So did Jesus' descent into Sheol (the Anastasis), which the Acts of Pilate, also known as the Gospel of Nicodemus, describe in graphic detail.

The almost novelistic character of the apocryphal books, and their overemphasis on the miraculous, rightly caused the church to deny them a place in the canon of Scripture. Some of their stories, told and retold through the centuries as pious legends, have a poetic charm that makes them enjoyable even today. They had sprung up like folk tales, their anonymous authors trying to give vent to a naïve and touching love for Christ and his mother. Yet when they received a prominent place alongside authentic Biblical narratives, it was often for the support of doctrines based on tradition rather than on Scripture. Protestants who accept only the latter as revealed truth regret the intrusion of so much apocryphal material and consider it harmful.

Byzantine art continued to adhere to the Mosaic law against the visual representation of God, admitting only the symbol of a hand extending from a cloud or aureole. When the need arose to illustrate the book of Genesis, Byzantine artists continued a solution found first on some early sarcophagi. It was to show the First Person of the Trinity in the form of Christ, in literal interpretation of John 12:45 ("He who sees me sees him who sent me") and Heb. 1:2. We see the youthful Creator on mosaics, wall paintings, book illuminations, ivory carvings, even the bronze doors of San Zeno in Verona.

During the Byzantine era more detailed Passion scenes and the crucifixion itself made their appearance in art. One of the earliest examples of the latter is preserved on the wooden doors of San Sabina, Rome, about 430. The famous Syrian Gospels written in 586 by the monk Rabula in Mesopotamia show the pattern that was to be regularly followed. (It may go back to an earlier mosaic, now lost, in the church on Mt. Zion in Jerusalem.) We see Christ on the cross, dressed in a long garment (the colobium), with Longinus piercing his side and Stephaton passing the sponge to his lips. The two thieves are crucified on Jesus' right and left. Three soldiers are casting dice for the seamless robe; the women and the disciple John stand by in sorrow. Christ's arms are stretched out horizontally, his body is upright; there is no attempt to convey a sense of physical suffering. The emphasis is entirely on the crucifixion as the means of redemption, not on a realistic representation of Christ's agonized death.

This period also saw the introduction of the Last Judgment theme in Christian art. The Ravenna mosaics had merely suggested the coming judgment in the panel of the separation of sheep and goats, after Matt. 26:31-33. Prior to the eleventh century, the theme in its apocalyptic version does not occur, doubtless because the church lived in the expectation that the year 1000 would see the fulfillment of the millennium and the Second Coming of Christ. After the date had passed, the church found it necessary to stress the doctrines of the resurrection of all flesh, and of judgment, heaven, and hell. Also, more and more detailed representations of the Last Judgment began to appear, designed, in the spirit of Dante's "Inferno" and "Purgatorio," as a warning for sinners to remember the just wrath of God. The oldest surviving example of major im-

portance is a large mosaic in the basilica of Torcello. Christ
is seated in glory with the Virgin Mary and John the Baptist
at his sides. With the apostles next to them and hosts of angels, they are watching the dead being called up and judged.
The elect look up in attitudes of prayer; the condemned sinners are already being swallowed up in a lake of fire. Little
blue devils swarm around them and turn them over to Lucifer,
who receives them sitting on a serpent throne. Additional
panels at the bottom show other sinners waiting for their punishment, dismembered limbs, and skulls through whose empty
eye sockets blue worms crawl. The whole composition is done
with great skill, but its effect today is more that of a nightmare
than of a serious call to repentance. A pattern was established
that was destined to be more fully developed as time went on.
Artists vied with one another in the increasingly realistic
depiction of the horrors meted out to the condemned. There
is scarcely a larger medieval church without a painting or
sculptured relief of the Day of Doom.

Byzantine art at its best reaches spiritual heights rarely if
ever surpassed. Its less admirable qualities, from the viewpoint
of our age, are a rigid adherence to conventions that, as we
know from the Painter's Book from Mt. Athos, prescribed the
execution of every detail and an often excessively ceremonial
character. It stemmed from the highly formalized ritual of the
court of an emperor or basileus who saw himself as Christ's
representative on earth. Byzantine mosaics and ivory carvings
sometimes show him and his wife seated next to the Savior,
or being personally crowned by him. The idea, wholly unacceptable to us, has now merely historical interest.

The art of northern and western Europe during the centuries of the migrations likewise has more aesthetic and historical than religious significance to us. It illustrates the struggle of the faith to overcome pagan beliefs. Earliest sculptured
crosses in Ireland occasionaly show hunting scenes, fabulous
animals, even a figure interpreted as an ancient deer god.
Beautifully illuminated manuscripts like the *Book of Kells*

abound in fantastic creatures. The so-called Frank's Casket in the British Museum, London, a box carved from whalebone probably in the eighth century, shows the adoration of the Magi next to scenes from the ferocious Northern saga of Ve- land the smith. Woodcarvings in Scandinavian churches con- tinue to illustrate pre-Christian mythological stories as late as the thirteenth century. The warlike spirit of the Germanic tribes was not easily subdued by the gentler teachings of the Christian faith. It betrays itself in their fascination with the one martial act in the New Testament, Peter's attack against the servant of the high priest in the Garden of Gethsemane. On the great choir screen of Naumburg Cathedral, carved about 1270, Peter wields a huge two-handed sword and has forced his opponent to his knees; the dramatic action almost obscures the main protagonists of the betrayal scene.

D. The Later Middle Ages

After the stabilization of Europe under Charlemagne and his successors, and the passing of the dreaded year 1000, a great upsurge in church building set in, and with it a tre- mendous growth of religious art. To the basilican ground plan of early Christian churches was added a transept (in some cases two) in order to have space for the side altars made nec- essary by the veneration of local saints and the custom of say- ing masses for the dead. The plan of the church then formed a cross. A passageway or ambulatory carried the aisles around the choir which developed when the central nave was con- tinued beyond the transept. It was often separated from the rest of the church by an elaborate choir screen. The addition of side chapels and of a crypt under the altar area, where rel- ics of a saint or martyr could be visited by pilgrims, completes the plan of the great majority of medieval churches and cathe- drals.

The Romanesque churches of the eleventh and twelfth cen- turies are usually heavy structures with thick walls and few, small windows. They offer ample space for mural paintings, which in western Europe replaced the much more costly and difficult mosaic technique, or for woven or embroidered wall hangings. The ceilings were at first of wood, but frequent conflagrations made stone vaulting far preferable. It took time and experience to advance from the heavy vaults, which gave the churches an overly massive and dark appearance, to lighter methods of vaulting. By the twelfth century the Romanesque style had conquered its problems of construction. The churches of this period are well lighted, harmonious, and of great clarity of design. Horizontal and vertical lines balance each other. The whole building gives an impression of worshipful simplicity and dignity.

The invention of the ribbed vault, with its supporting system of buttresses and "flying" buttresses, and the use of the pointed instead of the semicircular arch, brought about dramatic changes. Soon after 1150 vast, lofty structures in an entirely new style began to be built. It was not until almost four hundred years later, however, that this style received its name "Gothic" from the Italian painter Vasari. He coined it in remembrance of the sack of Rome by the Goths in 410, to express his thorough dislike of an architecture that he and most of his fellow countrymen thought uncouth and barbarous.

Yet technical innovations alone do not explain the new forms. They are the manifestations of a new spirit, a new religious experience that culminates in scholasticism and mysticism. From France, where the style was first developed, it swept across all of Europe. Horizontal lines have all but vanished. Towering verticals shoot up to dizzying heights, often without a single break. They force the eye upward to where the slender ribs leap toward each other until they touch, at the apex of the vault, like branches in an avenue of trees or like hands lifted high in prayer. Once the builders had fully mastered the new structural system, they began to lighten the walls until only huge windows seem to remain. Their stained glass transforms the interior into a mystic shrine glowing in deep, rich hues. In Chartres, Bourges, York, or wherever enough of the original glass has survived, the effect is like a transparent carpet of precious stones. Now one, now the other, flashes up in the light that then spreads a second carpet of living colors on the floor of the cathedral.

True stained-glass windows resemble mosaics in that they are put together of many pieces of glass of different colors. These are cut according to the design and are fitted together with strips of lead that weave a net of black lines across the window. It does not seriously affect figures of large size, but smaller scenes are often difficult to interpret.

At the height of its development the Gothic church resembles a vast glass cage. One marvels how the attenuated supports can hold up the vault that floats, almost weightless, high above the nave. The clue lies in the complex arrangement of buttresses, topped by slender pinnacles for additional weight, and steeply curved flying buttresses reaching across the roofs of aisles and ambulatory. Together with pointed gables, finials, and spires, they stress the uplift of the dominant vertical lines. Yet they also give the exterior of many Gothic buildings a skeletonlike appearance, or as if the scaffolding had been left standing. And since stained-glass windows look grayish-black from the outside, one can understand why the artists of the Italian Renaissance greatly preferred their own style whose logic and clarity had been inspired by ancient Roman architecture.

Among the many Gothic cathedrals there are no duplications; each has its unique characteristics. France built some of the largest and tallest. English cathedrals are usually longer and set amidst trees and lawns rather than in the center of busy cities. The Baltic region achieved striking effects through the use of brick instead of ashlar. Countless parish churches, too, often of sizable proportions and inspiring beauty (for instance, St. Mary Redcliffe in Bristol), and churches of various religious orders rose above the roofs of the medieval towns and villages from one end of Europe to the other. The aptly named "perpendicular" style in England and the "flamboyant" in France developed more and more complex forms of vaulting and window tracery until some late Gothic churches resemble lacework in stone. This overelaboration hastened the end of the Gothic style, though provincial builders held on to it until the seventeenth century. The first church built by English settlers in America, St. Luke's Parish in Virginia, still shows a simplified Gothic. Spain too had not yet abandoned the Gothic when Columbus reached Hispaniola in 1492, and when the cathedral of Santo Domingo was being built between 1521 and 1527, the first in the New World.

But the spirituality that had produced the Gothic style had vanished with the dawn of a new era. Fashionable Italian Renaissance forms came in, to be replaced in the seventeenth century by the muscularity of the baroque and, a hundred years later, the graceful, musical playfulness of the rococo. The Gothic seemed forgotten — until the romantic movement rediscovered it in the second half of the eighteenth century. A newly awakened enthusiasm for the Middle Ages led to a Gothic revival that also spread to America. Some of the churches built at that time have undeniable appeal. Soon, however, a dry academism and eclecticism took hold. Gothic forms translated into wood construction lost their functional purpose and were treated as mere decoration. Elements from various periods and regions were casually combined into a dispirited mixture, without the power to lift the spirit and to convince. Near the end of the nineteenth century, the gifted American architect Henry H. Richardson broke away from the stereotype and returned to the solid construction and rhythmical design of the Romanesque. Later architects endeavored to build in pure, undiluted Gothic, but in the long run these efforts proved unsatisfactory. Imitation of the past amounts to a confession that the religious life of the church has stagnated and lost the capacity for creative self-expression. Much as we admire the work of the Middle Ages, we no longer think and feel as they did. In many ways our faith differs from theirs.

The medieval churches spoke to the people not only through

the beauty of their structure. Equally important was the message conveyed in the visual language of paintings, sculptures, and other works of art. They were meant to instruct, exhort, persuade, console, even to entertain, and range from the sublime to the ridiculous, from the deeply spiritual to the grossly mundane. For the church was more than a place of worship. It had also assumed the functions of a center of learning, stage for the liturgical drama, shrine where the dead were laid to rest, and community center. "Parish churches and churchyards were used for community dancing, games, banquets, sports, buffoonery, festivals, fairs, and markets." [6]

Yet the medieval church was designed first and foremost as the setting for the daily celebration of the Mass. It can be fully understood only in reference to the belief in transubstantiation, the real presence of the crucified Lord on the altar when, after consecration by the priest, bread and wine change into the flesh and blood of the Savior. The doctrine had slowly developed from the Eucharistic meals of the early congregations. It was formally established by the fourth Lateran Council of 1215, and remains the cornerstone of the Roman Catholic and Orthodox liturgies.

The service of the Mass was seen both as a continued self-offering of the Redeemer and as an offering to God made by the priest on behalf of and in the name of the congregation. It recognized Christ's sovereign dominion over all created life. Every detail pertaining to it had to be ordered with greatest care as befitting its solemnity, and was replete with symbolic significance. As the churchmen of the Middle Ages pondered the mystery of the incarnate God, they discovered in sacred and profane history, in science and literature, in observed and fabled natural phenomena, and in the daily rhythms of human life, an inexhaustible wealth of parallels and allusions to which art could give visual form. The church thus became an encyclopedia, a *summa theologica,* for the glorification of God and the edification of the people.

To Christ as head of the church belonged the highest honors. His majestic image adorns the portal as a reminder of his word: " I am the door; if any one enters by me, he will be saved, and will go in and out and find pasture " (John 10:9). The symbols of the Evangelists surround him because we know him through their Gospels. In the judgment scene the elders of the apocalypse are listening to him while the dead are rising from their graves, either to enter heavenly bliss or to be enchained and led into the gaping mouth of Leviathan, symbol of hell.

Statuary, wall paintings, or stained-glass windows present the essential events in the life of Christ, with strong emphasis on the Nativity (i.e., the incarnation) and the Passion. Numerous scenes and single figures add the authority of the Old Testament. It was interpreted as a prefiguration of the New; Augustine had coined the phrase that the New Testament is hidden in the Old, the Old Testament revealed in the New. The search for more and more parallels became one of the major preoccupations of medieval Schoolmen. Their findings were gathered in widely used books such as the *Concordantia veteris et novi Testamenti,* written in the ninth century by Walafrid Strabo, and the *Mirror of the World* of Vincent of Beauvais. Later compilations, the popular *Biblia Pauperum* (Bible of the Poor) and the *Mirror of Human Salvation,* carried the attempts to discover anagogical or typological meanings in the Old Testament to extremes of casuistry. These books provided ample subjects for the artistic decoration of the churches, but by the time of the Protestant Reformation the whole approach had become irrational to the point of absurdity and defeated itself.

Patriarchs and kings were represented as prototypes of Christ, prophets because they were believed to have foretold his coming. We can understand Melchizedek's offering of bread and wine to Abraham as a prefiguration of the Eucharist, or Abraham's sacrifice of Isaac as a symbol of Christ's death on the cross. But who would know today that Absalom's revolt against David " signified " Judas' betrayal, or the women of Israel's coming out to greet David (I Sam. 18:7), Jesus' entry into Jerusalem? Diligent research in medieval theology has provided explanations for many of these farfetched illustrations, yet much still remains to be elucidated.

This is likewise true of the many prefigurations of the Virgin Mary "discovered" in the Old Testament. Near the end of the Middle Ages her position as bearer of the incarnate Word had come to equal, if not in some ways to surpass, that of Christ himself. Her life story, embellished by legends and apocryphal writings, provided art with a large variety of motives. The saints also assumed an ever-greater role in Christian art, both the great martyrs known throughout the Christian world and the local saints whose veneration had not spread beyond a particular area or locality. Like the Virgin Mary, the apostles, and other confessors of the faith, they were invoked by name during the service of the Mass, and their images joined the clouds of witnesses around the altar.

Symbolical interpretation of all of created nature brought the signs of the zodiac, the labors of the months, and a profusion of animal and plant life to the cathedral. The material world in all its manifestations was seen as a mirror of the spiritual, as "a great book written by the hand of God, in which every being is a word charged with meaning. The ignorant man sees only mysterious figures, letters whose meaning he cannot understand. But the wise man raises himself from the visible to invisible things. By studying nature he reads the thought of God himself. Knowledge consists not in the study of things as they are but in the understanding of God's teachings as revealed in all things. . . . The world of the mind and the world of the senses are one." [7]

Yet we wonder if the medieval artist was not sometimes just playful when he carved a cockfight on a capital, or acrobats and wrestlers, animal tamers, mermaids, hunting scenes, and amusing fables. Surely he enjoyed chiseling out those ferocious devils who gleefully rope in kings and high-ranking clergymen, or grab the soul of Dives (in the form of his nude body) to twist it into a pretzel. It is hard to imagine that the gargoyles and cynical monsters squatting on cathedral parapets and threatening to take off from their roosts were seriously believed to be demons chained to the church to ward off evil. And certainly the carvers of choir stalls, especially of the underseat supports, or *misericordiae,* designed inconspicuously to lighten the strain of standing up during the long services, must have had a great deal of fun as they allowed their fancy to roam freely, touched not infrequently with a robust sense of humor.

Scholars have found symbolic significance in the real or imagined creatures abounding in medieval art: elephants, griffins, unicorns, bears, lions, eagles, and all kinds of monsters. In the eyes of the theologians each had its special meaning, but the people probably thought most of them simply odd and entertaining. Bernard of Clairvaux vigorously attacked curious carvings and paintings that attract the worshiper's gaze and hinder his attention. "To what purpose," he asked, "are those unclean apes, those fierce lions, those monstrous centaurs, those half men . . . , those fighting knights, those hunters winding their horns? . . . For God's sake, if men are not ashamed of these follies, why at least do they not shrink from the expense?" [8]

Bernard's words come to mind when one visits the beautiful and inspiring Abbey Church of Vézelay in Burgundy, the very church where Bernard preached the second crusade in 1146. To the modern mind there is simply too much deviltry on the roughly carved capitals of the nave piers. Yet the same church preserves one of the masterpieces of medieval sculpture in the huge tympanum above the doorway leading from the narthex into the nave. Here Christ is seen sending out the apostles to witness for him "to the end of the earth" (Acts. 1:8). In its austere dignity, almost severity, his figure resembles the Pantocrator of the Byzantine mosaics, except that it shows a more intense emotion. The gestures and swaying garments of the apostles reveal their excitement on receiving the Holy Spirit,

symbolized by rays leading from Christ's hands to their heads.
(The relief has also been interpreted as the Pentecost.) On the
lintel below and on the archivolt framing the main composition appear strange-looking figures, the people "from the ends
of the earth," and the infirm in mind or body whom the
apostles will have power to heal. Here are visualized prophe-
cies of Isaiah (ch. 35:5-6 and ch. 66:19), which since Jerome's
time have been understood as foretelling the mission of the
apostles. The cosmic aspect of the tympanum is further en-
larged by the signs of the zodiac and scenes portraying the
occupations of the months. "Christ is not only the ruler over
space, over all the races of the world, but also over time, over
the cycle of the year and its activities." [9]

Less than half a century after the Vézelay tympanum had
been put in place, the stern, hieratic Romanesque style
changed to the graceful and refined Gothic. Sculptors and
painters from Cimabue, Duccio, and Giotto on, loosened the
rigidity inherited from Byzantine art. Like the statues adorn-
ing the great Northern cathedrals, their figures increasingly
take on the appearance of actual life, with garments following
the natural lines of the body and stressing its three-dimensional volume. Features become individualized; details of
costume and hair are rendered with careful observation. The
stirrings of scientific interest at the newly founded universities
combined with a new and far more favorable outlook on nature for which the teaching and example of Francis of Assisi
were probably the most significant moving force.

For centuries Christians had felt hostile toward nature because it too stood under the curse of the Fall. As long as all
flesh was held to be sinful, art purposely avoided any emphasis on physical beauty, lest it might lure the thoughts of the
faithful away from concentration on the spirit. Homeliness of
features was therefore preferred for the representation of
saintly personages. Their glance is directed inward rather than
outward. Their bodies almost disappear under stylized garments whose swirling, spiraling lines suggest the vehemence

of spiritual experience. Action and intent are indicated by telling gestures and emphatically pointed fingers.

All this now changed. The gentle friar from Assisi taught his
fellow men to look at nature with new eyes, to recognize in it
God's handiwork. Nature entered the temple of God in his
praise. Capitals and doorways of Gothic churches blossomed
forth with lovingly studied plants and flowers such as grew in
vineyards, woodlands, and gardens. Gothic manuscripts are
almost literally fragrant with the sweet smell of carnations
and violets. Statues of apostles and saints greet the worshiper
with a friendly smile as he enters the church, and accompany
him to the altar to tell him the story of salvation. Theologians
followed Thomas Aquinas in seeing the beauty of creation as
a likeness of divine beauty, and artists happily accepted the
new outlook.

The Gothic cathedrals create so grandiose an impression,
and their statuary and stained-glass windows breathe such
spiritual fervor, that the modern visitor is likely to be overwhelmed. Yet a nagging doubt persists. Does the worship of
God really demand what can only be called canyons of stone
and glass? Did the medieval builders strain every resource
purely to honor his name, and not also to satisfy their own
personal and civic pride? And when the Gothic sculptors and
painters bring the men and women of the Bible, and the saints,
so much closer to us, are they still capable of conveying the
poignant sense of awe before the unknowable, as earlier art
does? Byzantine and Romanesque art invite contemplation
and prayer; can we really say the same of the Gothic, with its
so much greater eye appeal? We must ask these questions and
answer them truthfully if we are to understand clearly the
real function and purpose of Christian art, and prepare the
ground for the new forms that the spiritual life of our own
time urgently demands.

As political and social conditions changed in the later Middle Ages, communal religious experience yielded its dominant
place to individual piety. Art developed aids to private devo-

tion and for a more personal and intimate approach to the sacred. Among them were the popular *Books of Hours* containing prayers for each part of the day. Whether they were luxurious work of court painters or mass-produced for the average citizen, they were generally interspersed with charming, colorful miniatures. Some of them were intended to elucidate the main theme of the prayer, others merely to entertain the eye while familiar words are being recited. Many a Flemish painting of the fifteenth century shows the Virgin Mary kneeling at her prayer desk reading in just such a book. (About this time the rosary too came into use as a prayer aid.) Small ivory tablets, hinged by twos or threes and showing scenes from the life of Christ or of the Virgin Mary, became the fashion for the home altars of the wealthy. From the fifteenth century on, the graphic arts provided large numbers of inexpensive woodcuts and engravings, allowing people of limited means to have a religious image in their homes. *Crucifixi* and other small works of art in a variety of materials served the same purpose.

Artists followed the trend to the intimate by making their forms more delicate and gracious and by emphasizing emotional expression. The Madonna, once the crowned and richly robed queen of heaven, a hieratic figure holding up the infant Savior for adoration, now became increasingly the human mother who tenderly smiles at her Son, a lovable, even cuddly child who caresses his mother or plays in childlike manner with a little bird. A statue of the Madonna or of a saint was often affixed to a house front or a public building to invoke protection. On crossroads, in fields and vineyards, similar figures, or the image of the crucified Christ, invited the people to pause, as they went their way, to say a prayer. Little wayside shrines of this kind are still a common sight in most Roman Catholic countries. They are rarely without some flowers laid down by pious hands. (PLATE 6)

The themes of many of these carvings in stone or wood, often touchingly naïve in their rustic simplicity, are derived from a group of devotional images that belong to the most moving works of late medieval art. They reflect the intense desire of the mystic writers and poets of the time for close spiritual union with the Savior through the contemplation of every aspect of his Passion. The *imago pietatis* shows Christ as the Suffering Servant of Isaiah: "He was despised and rejected by men; a man of sorrows, and acquainted with grief " (Isa. 53:3-5). The "Man of Sorrows" stands or sits alone, like a new Job, mourning the sins of the world. Blood runs from the wounds in his hands, feet, and side; the heavy crown of thorns presses upon his brow. Sometimes he stands in the open tomb with the cross and the instruments of the Passion, supported by the mournful figures of Mary and John, or by angels. In the *Ecce Homo* image, Christ is exposed, mocked, and scourged, his hands tied. Or he may be treading the "grapes of wrath" in the winepress (Rev. 19:15; Isa. 63:3), in symbolic reference to the life-giving power of the Eucharist. This motive retained its appeal in Reformation days. It occurs, for instance, on the title page of the large Elector's Bible of 1641.

The preoccupation with Christ's sufferings explains the almost ruthless realism of some *crucifixi* of the fourteenth and fifteenth centuries. It culminated in Mathias Nithard-Grünewald's *Crucifixion* scene from the Isenheim Altar of around 1517, now in the Unterlinden Museum at Colmar, Alsace. No artist has shown the reality of the Savior's death with a more relentless insistence on truth. The great painting sweeps aside all soothing platitudes and forces us virtually to become partakers of the Golgotha tragedy. Darkness has covered the sky as the Son of Man has breathed his last. His heavy body hangs, bruised and torn, on a roughly timbered cross. The sunken head, the wrenched shoulders, the hands and feet rigid in the twisted cramp of the last moments, seem to cry out, "My God, my God, why hast thou forsaken me?" (PLATE 7)

Through long, slow hours of bitter anguish Mary has stood by her Son and watched him die. Now she has fainted into the arms of the beloved disciple, who himself is overwhelmed with grief. Her infinitely telling hands remain tightly clasped as she has held them in ceaseless prayers. Mary Magdalene sobs heartbroken at the foot of the cross.

We would feel crushed by the terrifying power of this vision were it not for the firm assurance of John the Baptist. Miraculously risen from the grave, he points to Jesus with a compelling gesture: "He must increase, but I must decrease" (John 3:30). To dispel any doubt, the artist has painted in the words of the message. Golgotha, we are to remember, was not the end.

The soul-testing work asks the question we hear in the spiritual: "Were you there when they crucified my Lord?" Our generation, which has come to know boundless human suffering in the concentration camps, in the flaming nights of saturation bombing, in the holocausts of Hiroshima and Nagasaki, understands the depth of agony in Grünewald's painting. It is not surprising to find an echo of it in some of the most expressive modern versions of the crucifixion.

Another tragic image of medieval art, that of the *Pietà*, was also derived from the mystic poets. As they followed in spirit the events of Good Friday, it seemed natural to them that Mary must have wanted to take the body of her Son once more into her arms after it had been lowered from the cross, broken and disfigured by the signs of his sufferings. Thus in the *Pietà* we see Mary holding Christ on her lap as she had done so often when he was a child. The moving theme inspired Michelangelo to carve it several times in marble. Probably the best known of his groups is the one in St. Peter's in Rome, beautiful in its quiet sadness; but the versions in Florence Cathedral and in the Sforza Castello in Milan are more deeply felt. The latter had to be left unfinished by the aged master when death removed the chisel from his hand.

A place close to it must be given to the work of an unknown French painter of the fifteenth century. The *Pietà of Avignon* in the Louvre, Paris, will remain unforgettable to all who have stood before it in quiet meditation. The severe simplicity of its broken, angular lines, the convincing sincerity of its reverent mood, command silence. Mary's heroic figure, frozen in grief, asks the question inscribed across the panel: "Is it nothing to you, all you who pass by? Look and see if there is any sorrow like my sorrow" (Lam. 1:12). Few other works of Christian art have such power to stir us to compassion and a deeper realization of what Christ's death means to each one of us: "Greater love has no man than this, that a man lay down his life for his friends" (John 15:13). (PLATE 8)

Christ's resurrection, rarely shown in early Christian art, became a frequent theme in the Middle Ages. It occurs regularly in Bible and Psalter illustrations, on windows and altars. Unfortunately, the majority of these representations are disappointing. The event they try to visualize is too far above human understanding for an artist to do it justice in any but a symbolic manner. The Gospels wisely are restrained about it, and earlier painters and sculptors had followed their lead by passing directly from the entombment to the Easter morning scenes. Two paintings stand out from all others. Piero della Francesca's heroic fresco in Borgo San Sepolcro near Arezzo, Italy, shows Christ as he steps forth from the tomb, the flag of victory in his hand. His majestic figure is bathed in the light of dawn in token that a new day for mankind has begun. The strength and unity of the pyramidal composition, the elimination of unessential detail, the marvelous feeling of early-morning stillness, combine to suggest the breaking into this world of the supernatural. This deeply serious Christ has gone through the valley of the shadow of death and conquered its terrors. (PLATE 9)

Grünewald's *Resurrection* panel from the Isenheim Altar is a vision of light defeating darkness. An aureole like a sunburst surrounds the figure of Christ, radiant against the night sky. While the graveclothes are falling away, he soars upward, lifted by the same irresistible force that has brushed aside the heavily armed soldiers around the tomb. Almost smiling, he raises his hands to show the marks of his wounds, in a gesture that is both uplift and blessing. The mystic fervor of the North contrasts sharply with the lucid clarity of the South in these two masterpieces.

E. The Reformation Period

On October 31, 1517, Martin Luther affixed his ninety-five theses to the door of the palace chapel at Wittenberg. His anger had been aroused by the abuses connected with the sale of indulgences for the remission of sins, particularly during an intensive campaign to raise large sums of money for the rebuilding of St. Peter's. He had observed the extravagance of the papal court in Rome and was convinced of the pope's ability to finance an undertaking that Luther considered far too ambitious anyhow. Indulgences could also be earned by prayers before certain religious images, mainly of Passion scenes, some of which were claimed to be miracle-working. The widespread veneration of sacred images and relics, despite its repeated condemnation by church leaders and theologians, made all imagery highly suspect to the Reformers. Besides, the fundamental change in doctrine from the Mass to the Protestant Communion service deprived much of the artistic decoration of the churches of its full significance and made it distracting rather than helpful. When the Reformers opposed the belief in the intercessory powers of the Virgin Mary and the saints, their representation in works of art could be misleading and a hindrance to pure worship. As early as 1521–1522 the first image-breakings occurred in Wittenberg, though against Luther's will.

For neither Luther nor Zwingli was entirely hostile to religious art as such. They insisted on orderly removal of altar shrines, *crucifixi*, and statuary where it seemed necessary. Only images that had received popular veneration were to be destroyed. The arts, Luther reasoned, were a gift of God. It would be foolish to give up what could well serve to teach the faith, as long as it was not accorded unjustifiable honors. Stained-glass windows, for instance, ought to be retained, since hey had never been the object of devotion. But images that could tempt the credulous to idolatry, Ulrich Zwingli warned, should not be preserved. The bitter outcry against their removal proved to him that they meant more to their defenders than visual reminders of spiritual truths, and in the end he decided to renounce all images. It is worth noting, however, that many of his books and pamphlets appeared in print with woodcut illustrations. We find the Man of Sorrows, the crucifixion, the resurrection of the dead, and a print showing Christ with the cross in his hand surrounded by men and women who are shouldering their own crosses in an effective visualization of what Christ demands of his followers. Zwingli's own copy of the Bible had woodcut initials with scenes from sacred history. A wall catechism printed in Zürich in 1525 even presents the Decalogue held up by God. The use of such illustrations proves that fear of the veneration of images, not a rejection of religious art, motivated the iconoclasm of the Reformed church. Some of the title pages have typical Renaissance ornamental frames with the very monsters, fabled beasts, *putti,* and figures from classical antiquity against which the Reformers so strongly protested; obviously, the printer simply took what he had available in his stock.

Martin Luther's position was more tolerant. Unlike some extremists among his followers, he never assumed that the masses of churchgoers identified the image with the person portrayed and thus actually adored wood and stone. He fought against indulgences, the cult of relics, pilgrimages, and any undue luxury in the church because they were considered "good works" that could earn merit toward salvation. From his reading of Rom. 1:16-17 he had come to make salvation through faith alone the cornerstone of his teaching. It had caused him to move away from the Roman Church. However, as long as no false doctrine attached itself to religious images, Luther was ready to admit them. Was it not better, he protested, to show God creating the world, Noah building the ark, or other praiseworthy stories from Scripture, than purely

worldly subjects? "I wish to God one could persuade the gen-
tlemen, and the rich, to paint the whole Bible inside and outside their houses for everyone to see; that would be a Christian
undertaking." A man at prayer would quite naturally have in
his mind an image of Christ on the cross. How, then, could it
be sinful to have before one's eyes what was not sin to have in
one's heart? The eyes too should praise God and render thanks
to him. A painting of the Last Supper would be most fitting,
Luther wrote, on an altar or in some other place in the church.
As a sign or memorial of holy living, even a *crucifixus,* an image of the Madonna, or of a saint, may be valuable and should
be preserved.[10]

Luther was a lifelong friend of Lucas Cranach's, the outstanding Protestant painter who made numerous portraits of
the Reformer and the men of his circle. Luther was keenly
interested in providing well-illustrated Bibles for the use of
the people, though he demanded that the artist faithfully adhere to the text. Cranach helped fulfill Luther's wish. The Reformer, an enthusiastic friend of congregational singing, desired to put all the arts to the service of the Creator.

Thomas Münzer and John Calvin turned more radically
against the use of images. The Anabaptists of southern Germany renounced churches as houses of idolatry. Their emphasis on the "inner voice" made all signs and symbols useless
to them. The more aggressive among this group demanded
the destruction of all altars and images. Calvin's stand was
nearly as uncompromising. In the eleventh chapter of the
first book of his *Institutes of the Christian Religion,* he scath-
ingly denounces religious imagery as an impious lie, an absurd
and indecorous fiction. "Whatever statues are set up or pictures painted to represent God, are utterly displeasing to him,
as a kind of insult to his majesty." Images must needs lead to
idolatry regardless of "whether they worship the idol simply,
or God in the idol."

But Calvin did not wish to declare himself against all art.
"As sculpture and painting are gifts of God, what I insist for

is, that both shall be used purely and lawfully, that gifts which
the Lord has bestowed upon us, for his glory and our good,
shall not be preposterously abused, nay, shall not be perverted
to our destruction." Historical representations of an event are
useful for instruction and admonition, but not pictorial works
of art that merely exhibit bodily shapes and figures.[11] He advocated a return to the first five hundred years when a purer
doctrine kept the churches completely free of visible representation. This mistaken belief was due to his lack of familiarity
with the monuments of early Christian art.

When it came to demanding radical measures against the
abuses and untenable practices prevailing in some areas of
religious art, the Reformers minced no words. Most conspicuous was the far too prominent role played in painting and
sculpture by purely apocryphal miracles of the saints. One of
the major sources for them was the *Legenda Aurea* of Jacopo
da Voragine. The immensely popular compilation, among the
earliest books to come from the printing presses, mixed fact
and fiction indiscriminately and obscured the Christian witness
of the saints and martyrs behind spurious incidents and fantastic, though picturesque, miracles.

The church even condoned artistic concepts that were
clearly in conflict with Christian doctrine. Representations of
the Holy Trinity as a three-faced head, or as three-crowned
persons enthroned side by side, were rightly condemned by the
Reformers. Paintings of the annunciation to Mary where a tiny
infant floats down toward her on rays of gold look naïve and
charming to us, but convey a false idea of the incarnation.
In the Mass of St. Gregory, a very frequent subject in fifteenth-
century art, Christ as Man of Sorrows stands on the altar as if
he were alive, suggesting a literal interpretation of the doctrine of his living presence in the sacrament.

The zeal of the Reformers was doubtless fanned by the hu-
manization of art brought about by the rediscovery of Roman
sculpture, mythology, and philosophy. Sacred personalities no
longer appeared as timeless symbols of great truths but as

men and women exactly like those one could meet in life, though perhaps of idealized beauty. The Madonna was now an attractive young woman kneeling in her immaculately clean bedroom, her mantle draped in carefully arranged folds around her shoulders. Jan van Eyck shows her presenting the infant Jesus to the ducal chancellor Rolin in an airy hall, and only the angel's holding a crown above Mary's head prevents the painting from coming close to a family portrait. At other times she presides over a donor's entire family, and not one of them even looks at her. In the popular pictures of the " Holy Kinship " we see a group of men, women, and children, modishly dressed middle-class people, yet they are meant to represent Mary, Joseph, Jesus, and their relatives. In Botticelli's *Adoration of the Magi,* members of the Medici family have replaced the Wise Men from the East. Ghirlandajo's *Birth of John the Baptist* treats the subject as an occasion to celebrate the beautiful Giovanna Tournabuoni. She has condescended to pay her respects and looks out at us from the center of the fresco (in the choir of Sta. Maria Novella, Florence) fully conscious of her noble rank. Numerous other examples could be cited where sacred history has been turned into a pretext for the display of fashion and elegance, and the glorification of prominent individuals.

A realistic style has to be handled with great care or it will diminish the spiritual message of a work of art. When the newly perfected technique of oil painting enabled artists to bring out the most minute details, their loving observation of the microcosm of nature was an act of homage to the Creator. Every flower and leaf, every wrinkle in a man's face, spoke to them of God, who, as Jesus told his disciples, had numbered the hairs on their heads. (Matt. 10:30.) Thanks to their humbly grateful approach, convincingly felt in the works of the Flemish, French, and German painters of the fifteenth century, the viewer is moved to meditate on this truth. This technique reached perhaps its greatest height in Hugo van der Goes's *Adoration of the Shepherds,* now in the Uffizi Gallery in Florence, one of the gems of Christian art of all times. (PLATE 10)

There is no worldliness in this Nativity scene, no self-conscious sophistication masquerading as piety. Joseph is a solid master craftsman, an unassuming, kindly person who has thought much and puts his humble trust in God. Mary has none of the idealized charm of so many other Madonnas. Her face and hands are those of a woman familiar with hardship and toil, but her reverent expression is ennobled by the sincerest, most unselfish love.

Yet the really astonishing feature of the thoughtful work is the three shepherds whose rough, weather-hardened faces and hands speak eloquently of their labors in the fields. One of them, a simple-minded man, can only stare in openmouthed admiration, hat in hand. Another makes an instinctive gesture as if he wanted to take up the infant and shelter him like a newborn lamb. His gentle features are transfigured by an inner light, the light of the pure in heart when they behold the glory of God.

The lovely angels, messengers from another sphere, do not hesitate to kneel close to the poor, unkempt shepherds. And much is offered to those who know the language of symbols: the columbines with their seven blossoms stand for the seven gifts of the Spirit, the iris for the grief Christ's mother will have to bear, the sheaf of wheat for the Eucharist. The harp over the doorway in the background is a sign that Bethlehem was the city of David, Jesus' ancestor.

As we grasp the meaning of this masterpiece, we share an insight that the painter may well have gathered from a passage in Thomas à Kempis' *Imitation of Christ:* " God walked with the simple people and showed himself openly unto the meek. He gave understanding unto them that were poor in spirit, and he hid his grace and secrets from them that were proud, high, and curious." [12] Our thoughts go to the Sermon on the Mount and the Beatitudes. When Christ called the meek and the poor in spirit blessed, did he remember his mother's telling him how they came to him when others did not, how they alone, to paraphrase a modern spiritual, knew from the beginning who he was?

Enough great examples of the realistic style exist — works by such masters as Donatello and Claus Sluter, Masaccio and Dürer, to name only a few outstanding men of this period — to prove that not style or technique alone but the depth and sincerity of the artist's vision are the decisive factors. This vision, however, was now turning away from the transcendental under the impact of vast changes in the political, social, and economic life. New scientific and geographical discoveries necessitated a radical revision of the world view of earlier times. Renewed familiarity with Greek and Latin writers, and ancient art and mythology, brought about a considerable laxity in the religious life of the educated groups. Much of what the church was teaching seemed old-fashioned or doubtful to enlightened minds. Some artists, disturbed by the trend, raised their voices in a protest similar to that of the fiery monk, Savonarola. The Dutch painter Jerome Bosch castigated the folly of a world drifting away from God; his ghastly visions of hell were painted as warning signals. The "Dance of Death," best known through Hans Holbein's woodcut series, reminded a hedonistic age of the briefness of man's days on earth. Many a *memento mori,* and the popular book *Art of Dying Well,* echoed the somber notes of the famous mystery play *Everyman.* But these voices were little heeded by those who were interested only in pleasure. For centuries the arts had stood almost exclusively in the service of the faith; now secular subjects gained the ascendancy. Portraits of individuals no longer contained a reference to religion. The gods of the pagan world rose once again in their enticing beauty — Venus, Mars, Apollo, Flora, Amor, Pan. Sensuality, thinly disguised, entered even the religious realm. Painters thought nothing wrong in having their mistresses pose as models for the Virgin Mary; saints were shown so lightly dressed as to provoke some of John Calvin's most spirited attacks.

We usually overlook the fact that the majority of the paint-

ings and sculptures of this period in the art galleries or still
in the churches for which they were made are of average or
poor artistic quality. A subject that can be inspiring when
treated by a great artist becomes dry and routine in the hands
of his followers and imitators, likely to appear staged, pretentious, or extravagant. Great talents too can succumb to this
danger when tempted to produce too much. A mannered emotionalism without strength then replaces real feeling, or an
elegance hardly capable of conveying a true sense of the
sacred. We can see it exemplified in the work of Raphael. The
early *St. Michael* in the Louvre seems to perform a courtly
dance; *St. Sebastian* (in Bergamo) holds an arrow as a refined lady would hold a demitasse. The ceiling of the Camera
della Segnatura in the Vatican shows a frankly seductive Eve.
The large frescoes in this room, where the popes affixed their
signatures to documents affecting the life of the church, give
equal space and importance to the Muses and Apollo on Mt.
Parnassus, to the philosophers of the School of Athens, and to
the glorification of the sacrament of the Eucharist. The beauty
of parts of the latter, mistakenly called the *Disputa,* scarcely
compensates for its over-all effect of staged display. Christ's
face is marred by oversweetness. The prophets and apostles
seated on the cloud bank below pay little attention to him;
one has folded his hands over his crossed legs and looks as if
he were bored.

Even Raphael's strongest religious works, the cartoons for
the tapestries to the life of Jesus and Paul, are often disturb-
ingly close to the theatrical, especially the *Death of Ananias.*
His designs for the Loggie in the Vatican, illustrating scenes
from the Old Testament, have a fairy-tale quality dangerously
skirting sacrilege in the representation of God the Father.
(The actual frescoes were painted by his pupils.)

Raphael's Madonnas have gained enormous popularity for
their refined beauty. In some of them the artist certainly struck
a worshipful note. Others, however, have too much physical
charm to evoke a sense of the mystery of the incarnation. The

Madonna of the Chair in the Pitti Palace, Florence, is a case in point. The solid realism of the figures, their exuberant vitality, glorifies the humanity of this young mother and her child, but leaves no room for the transcendental. To classify such Madonnas as outstanding examples of religious art is to read more into them than an unprejudiced observer is likely to see. The legacy of their overly idealized beauty, worlds apart from the humble "handmaiden of the Lord" in Hugo van der Goes's painting, has plagued Christian art for centuries. Raphael was undoubtedly at heart a secular artist. His mind was nourished by the philosophy and poetry of the age of humanism. He achieved complete success when he was free to deal with purely secular themes. The *Triumph of Galatea*, the designs for the story of Amor and Psyche in the Villa Farnesina, Rome, and his portrait paintings show him at his best.

Leonardo da Vinci's foremost concern was with artistic and scientific rather than with religious problems. He saw in *The Last Supper*, painted between 1495 and 1497 in the refectory of Sta. Maria della Grazie in Milan, an opportunity and challenge to work out a superbly balanced arrangement of figures at a moment of high tension. When the monks gathered for their meals it must have looked to them as if Christ and his disciples were physically present at the head table, so completely convincing is the painter's handling of perspective. Unfortunately, his experiments with pigments soon proved a failure. The painting deteriorated rapidly, requiring repeated restorations. It escaped destruction when the convent was leveled during an air raid on Milan, and has since been most carefully cleaned and repaired. But the face of Christ has remained the pale shadow it had been for a long time.

No other work of Christian art has achieved the renown of Leonardo's *Last Supper*. Millions of Christians visualize the event in terms of this painting, familiar through countless reproductions in every conceivable material, including marble and cork. They are generally made from old copies because of

the ruined state of the original. That it belongs among the
great creations of all times is incontestable. Yet we cannot but
regret the discouraging effect of its fame on other artists, for
no single version of the event can exhaust its implications. The
range of any artist's vision, even one as comprehensive as
Leonardo's, is of necessity limited by his time and place and
the exigencies of a particular situation. When one writer
states, in words intended as high praise: "In his creation of
the characters of the apostles, in the enigma of Christ's re-
signed silence, [Leonardo] concentrated centuries of Mediter-
ranean civilization characterized by its cult of man and of God
made human," [13] these limitations are put in clear relief. For
neither the faith of earlier periods of Christian history, nor
that for which our time strives again, can be described as a
"cult of man and of God made human."

The tragedy of Michelangelo, on the other hand, lies in his
titanic struggle to break through all limits and reach universal
truth. Solitary, frequently out of tune with his environment,
he saw with utmost clarity the dilemma of man's life. Created
in the image of God, he remains forever tied to the earth, to
sin and death. The glimpse of the infinite vouchsafed to him
makes his own finite existence the harder to bear. This dichotomy dominates Michelangelo's Medici tombs in Florence as
well as his grandiose ceiling frescoes in the Sistine Chapel in
Rome.

These scenes breathe the epic spirit of the first chapters of
Genesis. In the stories of the Creation, the Fall, and the Flood,
Michelangelo recognized man's attempt to express deepest insights into the nature of the divine-human encounter through
the poetic language of the myth. But while words point beyond themselves and can lead our searching minds to soar until we either lose ourselves or humbly confess that we can only
see "in a mirror dimly," the painter must of necessity use
forms and lines that limit the unlimitable. Thus, even Michelangelo had to envisage God in man's image. The awesome
mystery of the Eternal remains undisclosed, and what we see

is merely a magnificently conceived Zeus.

Michelangelo's true greatness is most fully revealed in the towering figures of prophets and sibyls in the same chapel, heroic symbols of men and women of God. They were closer to the artist's heart than was the person of Jesus Christ. The two statues he did of Jesus are unconvincing, to say the least. And when, much later in life, he painted the huge *Last Judgment* on the altar wall of the Sistine Chapel, he had become embittered by the worldliness he had observed at the center of the church, and by his own endless frustrations and disappointments. The athletically built Christ commanding the dead to rise seems far more eager to condemn than to pardon. Was Michelangelo affected by the sharply critical thinking of the Reformers? Did he wish to give stern warning when he placed, at the exact spot where the priest officiating at the altar must have it before his eyes, the image of a fierce devil smiting the sinners?

Neither the Reformers nor the two leading German artists sympathetic to their cause, Dürer and Cranach, visited the Sistine Chapel. Albrecht Dürer never met Luther personally, but he admired him greatly and offered to paint his portrait " as a lasting memory of the Christian man who has helped me out of great anxieties." Later he wrote that he and his friends had been sneered at as heretics, and he died a good Lutheran.[14] A long entry in the diary he kept during his journey to the Netherlands reveals how aggrieved he was when news reached him that Martin Luther had been taken prisoner on his return from the Diet of Worms. He could not know that it was a stratagem designed to ensure Luther's safety.

Dürer had always been close to the Bible. His large woodcuts on The Revelation to John are still the most forceful artistic interpretations of that book. His many scenes from the life of Christ and of Mary are serious and reverent. After his conversion to Lutheran thought he gave up almost entirely the subjects from classical antiquity that had played a considerable role in his earlier work and concentrated more and more on religious subjects "of a strictly evangelical character. The lyrical and visionary element was suppressed in favor of a Scriptural virility which ultimately tolerated only the apostles, the Evangelists, and the Passion of Christ." A woodcut of the Last Supper changes the establishment of a sacred ritual into the institution of the evangelical community. The altarlike table on which only the chalice is present emphasizes the Lutheran view of the Lord's Supper.[15]

Dürer's work culminated in the two panels of John and Peter, Mark and Paul (called *The Four Apostles*). The characterful heads and energetic figures of the men of faith proclaim the same dedication to the cause of Christ as Luther's great hymn, "A Mighty Fortress Is Our God."

Lucas Cranach had started out as a painter in the Catholic tradition of the time. Some of his early works are of the kind the Reformers were to condemn. He was Martin Luther's fellow townsman and became one of his closest personal friends and partisans. In paintings, woodcuts, and engravings he provided numerous portraits of the Reformer that enjoyed great popularity. Undiscouraged by the strong current of opposition to religious imagery in the new church, he set out to create a Protestant art. There was also the need for propaganda and attack, and a bold woodcut on the title page, somewhat resembling our political cartoons, was sure to attract more attention to a pamphlet.

Cranach and other artists used this vigorous technique to drive home highly charged accusations against the Roman church and its defenders, and against factions within the Reformed church. The opposition answered in kind, and we have the deplorable spectacle of mutual hatred and slander among professed Christians who persecuted one another from one end of Europe to the other and afterward in the American colonies. Some of these woodcuts are expressive enough to incite emotions to fever pitch, given the all-important place of the confessions at this time, but the majority are crude and can scarcely claim artistic, much less inspirational, value.

It was different with the illustrations to the Bible. As translations into the native languages came into print and were eagerly bought, graphic representations helped the readers to visualize the historic events and explain them to children and to the illiterate. Protestants as well as Catholics developed entire cycles of such illustrations. They were also used for hymnals, printed sermons, etc. Cranach, Holbein, Duvet, and others contributed outstanding designs which were reprinted again and again for centuries. Religious art thus retained a place as a servant of the Word even in churches that banned it from the house of God. (PLATE 11)

Lucas Cranach also painted a number of Protestant altar pieces. He preferred two main themes. One was the appealing scene of Christ blessing little children; the other, the story of man's temptation, fall, and expulsion from Paradise, contrasted with his redemption through Christ's death and resurrection. It is often extended to include the scenes of Moses receiving the Tablets of the Law and of the Last Judgment. The composition became so crowded with incident that it had to be explained at length by means of inscriptions. It did not congeal into a satisfying image because it tried to do too much at once. The theme of the blessing of little children, practically unknown in art before Cranach, was meant to underline Luther's principle of infant Baptism. It helped to replace the older concept of Christ as a stern ruler with the image of the loving friend of man, the gentle teacher. It brought the Savior right into the homes of the faithful, for the mothers pressing around him with their babies and infants wear the dress of the painter's time. The disciples are relegated to a small corner; their frowning disapproval only strengthens the message of the picture.

In the altar triptych for the city church of Wittenberg, Cranach painted the Last Supper unmistakably as a Communion service. On the wings Melanchthon baptizes a child, Bugenhagen accepts confession. The bottom panel (or predella) shows Luther preaching from the pulpit to an attentive con-

gregation of men, women, and children. He presents in his
sermon the crucified Christ, whom we see in the center. Another altar, in a church in Weimar, is like a synopsis of Reformation doctrine. Christ hangs on the cross. Blood spurts
from his side onto three figures standing on the right: John
the Baptist, who points to Jesus as the bringer of redemption;
Luther, with the open Bible; and old Lucas Cranach himself,
hands folded in prayer. At the foot of the cross stands the
lamb; to our left the risen Christ steps victoriously on death
and the devil. In the background the same two specters chase
man toward his grave; Moses erects the serpent of brass among
the tents of the Israelites and shows the people the Tablets of
the Law. Finally, in the far distance, the angel announces to
the shepherds the birth of the Savior. With all respect for the
sincerity of the painter's faith, we must admit he lacked the
artistic power to forge the many disparate motives into visual

unity. Overburdened with literary content, the work remains
a painted sermon.

F. After the Reformation

Lutheranism passed rapidly through the stage of iconoclasm
and, like Anglicanism, when taking over existing churches in
its territory, preserved many of their artistic treasures. Destruction of religious images continued spasmodically in those
areas where a strict Calvinism or Zwingli's Reformed church
prevailed. Innumerable works of medieval art were thus lost.
Some wall paintings, fortunately, were only covered with
whitewash and have of late come to light again. Recently a
ceiling painted with the sacrifice of Cain and Abel was rediscovered in the house of John Knox in Edinburgh. The new efforts, predominantly by Lutherans, produced few works of
more than provincial quality. Protestant sponsors increasingly
availed themselves of the services of Catholic artists and vice
versa, particularly after the Roman Catholic Church had realized the urgent need for a thorough revision of existing practices.

At its session of December 3, 1563, the Council of Trent accepted firm rules for religious art. It strongly supported the use of images " not because of a belief that they possessed divine power for the sake of which they had to be venerated, or because one could ask favors from them, or because one put confidence in them as of old the heathen had done, but because the honor shown to images returns back to their prototypes." Religious art could instruct the people and confirm them in the doctrines of the faith. In the images of the saints the faithful had before them examples for which to praise God and which they should imitate in their own lives. Lewdness was to be avoided; neither luxuriant beauty nor anything profane or immodest should appear in the house of God. New, unusual representations required the permission of the appropriate authorities of the church.

The Council of Trent heralded the so-called Counter-Reformation. It changed the outlook of the Roman Catholic world and brought about a new fervor. The baroque style of the sixteenth and seventeenth centuries was the expression of this spirit. Rejuvenated and once again sure of itself, the Roman Church, strongly aided by the newly founded Society of Jesus (the Jesuits), built churches and chapels resplendent with gold, marble, and color. They were decorated with large altarpieces and painted ceilings where Christ reigned in glory, or where the Virgin Mary, after her assumption, received a crown from the hands of her Son. Michelangelo's larger-than-life figures with their complex postures were freely imitated or adapted, though many of his followers succeeded only in creating declamatory and bombastic compositions. The typical church of the baroque style enfolds the worshiper in an ecstatic movement of colors and lines sweeping upward with a flutter of angels and the transfixed glances of saints to a vision of heavenly bliss. Even the straight lines of the walls disappear. Round or oval spaces merge into each other as if in one great outburst of joy. Ornamentation in bright hues adds to the festive music. In Austria, Bohemia, and southern Germany, but also in Italy, Spain, and Latin America, the style achieved triumphs of unified architectural and decorative planning of striking emotional impact.

The leading painters of the time — Titian, Tintoretto, El Greco, Rubens — received commissions for work on the largest scale. Scenes from the Old and New Testaments and the lives of saints as well as elaborate allegories came from their studios in rapid succession. The church also demanded realistic representations of martyrdoms. They were to be shown in all their horror, for the sufferings of the saints were believed to reflect glory on the church and to incite in the faithful the same courage to face death. In the paintings of Jusepe Ribera, or in Llano y Valdes' *San Fulgenzio* in the Vatican Gallery — a picture of a severed head, bleeding profusely — not even the most gruesome details were spared. The Madonna, on the other hand, was shown in radiant beauty. A favorite theme was the immaculate conception, widely accepted by the church long before it was declared dogma in 1854. Murillo's often repeated canvases established a definite pattern for it. Their all too obvious sweetness, once greatly admired, exudes a cloying sentimentality. The same is true of Carlo Dolci, Pierre Mignard, and a host of other artists of the Roman Catholic Church whose now almost unbearable overidealization catered to a popular taste. Reproductions of their works are still being sold and can be found on Christmas cards, calendars, and the like.

The intensely realistic style of Caravaggio was a sharp reaction against the vogue for glamorized piety. It met with disapproval by the church, but deeply influenced a number of painters both in Italy and abroad. Caravaggio was unorthodox in his insistence on visual truth and apparently in his religious views as well. He belonged to the circle of the well-loved Roman mystic, Filippo Neri, whose " low church" movement was close enough to Protestant views to be suspected of heresy. Caravaggio's paintings have the naturalness and intimacy of Filippo Neri's teaching and aim at a "direct com-

Plate 1   THE GOOD SHEPHERD: Marble. *Early Christian, ca. 300.*
Lateran Museum, Rome. [Photo courtesy Metropolitan
Museum of Art, New York City.]

Plate 2 Sarcophagus Front, The Mission to the Apostles: Marble. *Early Christian, ca. 385/390.* Milan, San Ambrogio. [Photo Pont. Comm. di Archeologia Sacra, Rome.]

Plate 3 MONREALE CATHEDRAL, INTERIOR TOWARD THE EAST: Mosaics. *After 1175.*

Plate 4 CHRIST PANTOCRATOR: Mosaic. *Between 1150 and 1200.* Cefalu Cathedral.

Plate 5   VIRGIN AND CHILD WITH TWO SAINTS: Ivory. *Byzantine, ca. 950–1000.* [Photo courtesy Dumbarton Oaks Collection, Washington, D. C.]

Plate 6 THE MADONNA OF DANGOLSHEIM: Wood. *Strasbourg Master, ca. 1470/1480*. Formerly Deutsches Museum, Berlin. [Photo Marburg Kunstinstitut.]

Plate 7 THE CRUCIFIXION: *Mathias Grünewald, German, ca. 1475–1528.* From the Isenheim Altar, ca. 1517. Unterlinden Museum, Colmar. [Photo Marburg Kunstinstitut.]

Plate 8   THE PIETA OF AVIGNON: *Unknown French Painter, ca. 1460. Louvre, Paris.* [Photo Archives Photographiques, Paris.]

Plate 9   THE RESURRECTION: Fresco, ca. 1460. *Italian, 1410/1420–1492.* Town Hall, Borgo San Sepolcro.

Plate 10 THE ADORATION OF THE SHEPHERDS: Center Panel, Portinari Triptych, ca. 1475. *Flemish, ca. 1440–1482.* Uffizi, Florence. [Photo Anderson.]

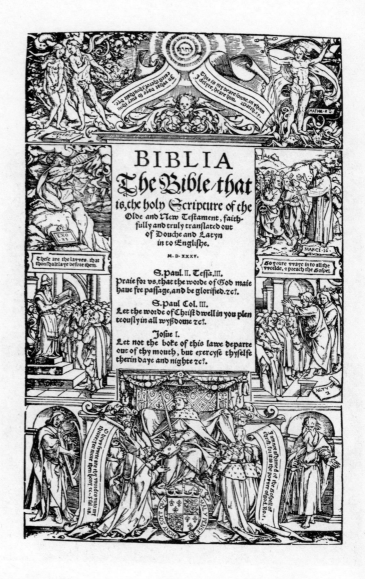

Plate 11   TITLE PAGE OF FIRST PRINTED ENGLISH BIBLE: *Coverdale's Translation, 1535.* [Photo courtesy British Museum, London.]

Plate 12 ABRAHAM'S SACRIFICE: Etching. *Rembrandt, Dutch,*
1606–1669. [Photo courtesy Boston Museum of Fine
Arts.]

Plate 13   HEAD OF CHRIST: *Rembrandt, ca. 1650–1665.* [Photo courtesy Metropolitan Museum of Art, New York City. Bequest of Isaac D. Fletcher, 1917.]

Plate 14 The Peaceable Kingdom: *Edward Hicks, American, 1780–1849.* [Photo courtesy Worcester, Mass., Art Museum.]

Plate 15　The Ascension of Christ: Water Color. *William Blake, British 1757–1827.* [Photo courtesy Fitzwilliam Museum, Cambridge.]

Plate 16 WHEN THE MORNING STARS SANG TOGETHER: Water
Color. *William Blake*. [Photo courtesy Pierpont Morgan
Library, New York City.]

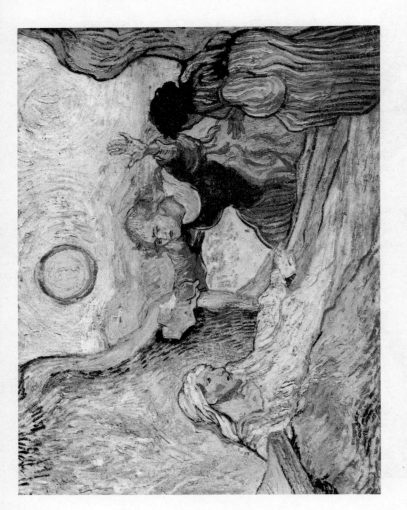

Plate 17   THE RAISING OF LAZARUS: 1890. *Vincent van Gogh, Dutch, 1853–1890.* [Photo courtesy Municipal Museum, Amsterdam.]

Plate 18 THE GOOD SAMARITAN: *Heinrich Nauen, German, born 1880.* [Photo courtesy Yale University Art Gallery, Collection Société Anonyme.]

Plate 19 THE CRUCIFIXION: Fresco, 1947. *Graham Sutherland, British, born 1903.* St. Matthew's, Northampton. [Photo courtesy British Information Services.]

Plate 20 ECCE HOMO, 1944. *Umberto Romano, American, born 1905.* [Photo courtesy of the artist.]

Plate 21   SOMETIMES THE BLIND HAVE COMFORTED THOSE WHO
SEE: Etching. *Georges Rouault, French, 1871–1958.*
[Photo courtesy Museum of Modern Art, New York City.]

Plate 22 SOLACE: Aquatint. *Karl Schrag, American, born 1912.*
[Photo courtesy of the artist.]

Plate 23 MAN FACING ETERNITY: Terracotta, 1954. *Charles Um-lauf, American, born 1911.* [Photo courtesy of the artist.]

Plate 24　Rest in the Peace of His Hands: Bronze, 1936. *Käthe Kollwitz, German, 1867–1945*. [Photo courtesy Wallraf-Richartz Museum, Köln.]

Plate 25 AMERICAN PIETA: *Tom Loftin Johnson, American, born 1900. Carnegie Institute, Pittsburgh.* [Photo courtesy of the artist.]

munication between the human being and the divine through faith." [16]

Protestant art of northern Europe had felt the impact of the Italian Renaissance and was willing also to adopt the new artistic forms for its own purposes. As the early Christians had taken over the style of pagan Roman art and filled it with new content and meaning, so the evangelical churches began to make use of the baroque, though generally in a sober, almost prosaic vein. The far greater importance of the sermon in Protestant worship required open, hall-like churches permitting as many people as possible to hear and see the preacher, while the plans of the Catholic churches favored individual worship at separate altars. In Reformed church buildings the altar, no longer the place of sacrifice, changed into a simple Communion table. Some of the sects, particularly the Friends (Quakers), abolished both altar and pulpit when they abandoned the professional priesthood, and purposely kept their houses of worship severely plain.

Lutherans, Anglicans, and to a lesser degree the Reformed church continued the use of paintings and statuary. As their artists followed the baroque style, it is sometimes difficult to recognize the Protestant character of a work until one studies the subjects represented. Instead of the saints called upon for intercession, we find the Passion and resurrection of Christ, scenes from the Old Testament, the apostles, allegorical figures of the virtues, and such ancient symbols as the pelican feeding his young with his own blood and the phoenix, symbol of the resurrection. Toward the end of the sixteenth century, large, complex altar retables came into fashion, with numerous individual scenes and the portraits of the donor and his family with his coat of arms. These retables look overloaded and too ornate. They impress more by sheer bulk than by their elaborate details.

Similar themes found a place on the richly decorated pulpits with their finely carved sounding boards. "The sumptu-

ous ornamentation of the pulpit is the artistic expression of the
value the evangelical church attributes to the sermon. . . .
The word of God as laid down in the Scriptures and mediated
by prophets and apostles . . . is the theme of the representations on the pulpits." [17] Baptismal fonts, ceilings, organ pros-
pects, and the enclosures of the galleries gave additional opportunities to instruct the congregation by means of paintings
or relief sculpture.

We must also mention the sculptured tombs and epitaphs
that began to fill the churches. Since medieval times some of
the greatest artists had created such monuments, either free
standing or affixed to a wall. Simple bronze, brass, or stone
slabs with the portrait of the deceased no longer satisfied the
demand for showy decoration. A full-length, three-dimensional
effigy of the dead person presents him as if asleep, his hands
folded. Angels hold his insignia of rank; lions or unicorns, his
coats of arms. Or the deceased was portrayed kneeling in
prayer before a crucifix, the Madonna, or his patron saint.

Then death itself made its appearance on the tombs. Skeletons warn the viewer: "What I am, thou shalt be, too." Protestantism fell in step with the trend toward the macabre. On
many a Puritan tombstone in New England churchyards, local
carvers chiseled winged skulls or entire skeletons. Sometimes
death "snuffs out the candle," a motive also found in a dramatic composition by the Spanish painter Valdes Leal. Fu-
nerals became the occasion for elaborate pomp, though none
of the funerary paintings mentioned in New England have
survived. We today find it strange that Christians should have
emphasized the physical aspects of death, not the hope of
resurrection.

We cannot sympathize, either, with the vanity displayed on
many epitaphs in European churches. The long, obsequious
inscriptions with their fulsome praise for the deceased, the
trophies, the scantily clad female figures posing as Justice,
Charity, Fortitude, or Fame, would seem to us in questionable
taste. Though some of these monuments have historical value

and may show refinement and a true sense of compassion, they are generally too conspicuous in the church not to distract the worshiper. They also often lack the spirit of humility befitting those who enter the house of God, whether in person or in effigy.

Here again Protestants fell in line with the artistic trends of the late Renaissance and baroque. The impact of Michelangelo's Medici tombs in the new sacristy of San Lorenzo, Florence, must have been a contributing factor. The four nude figures of Day and Night, Dawn and Dusk, on the large sarcophagi — which were left entirely without inscriptions — reveal a tragic vision of life. Their grandeur compares with the supreme works of classical antiquity, but their spirit is not Christian. It should not be overlooked that they are placed in a mausoleumlike room which was not designed for worship.

In sculpture, too, Michelangelo's tremendous force was changed by his followers into pathos and display. The height of this development was reached with Bernini's translation of Michelangelo into the full baroque. For his papal monuments in St. Peter's, Rome, he used tons of white and colored marble combined with bronze. Sensuous, feminine, allegorical figures are considerably less fully clothed than the present rules for visitors prescribe; death as a skeleton plays a prominent role. The over-all effect is one of incredible virtuosity on the part of the sculptor, but also of pomp and insincerity. For Urban VIII was decidedly not known for justice, and his charity went mainly to members of his own family. The monument occupies a niche near Bernini's towering glorification of Peter's Chair, a work that Protestants will find very difficult indeed to appreciate. Yet Bernini's influence reached far and wide and affected many a monument in the Protestant churches of the seventeenth century as well as the almost incredible Huguenot fountain at Erlangen, Germany, complete with allegorical figures, nude classic gods, and the Huguenots themselves.

In striking contrast, the same century produced in Rembrandt the greatest religious painter of Protestantism, if not of all Christianity. A son of Calvinist Holland, he was brought up to know and love the Bible. From his earliest beginnings as an artist to his last days it inspired him to memorable paintings, etchings, and drawings. There is scarcely a book of the Bible, including the Apocrypha of the Old Testament, such as Tobit, for which he did not design at least some illustrations. Several times Rembrandt Bibles have been published in recent years. The large proportion of religious subjects in his work is remarkable in view of the commonly held belief that the Calvinist Dutch were averse to religious images. While neither Rembrandt nor his followers received commissions for altarpieces, as did Rubens a few miles to the south in Antwerp, the Dutch people were by no means entirely opposed to having pictures with Biblical scenes in their homes. They also liked paintings of church interiors, the specialty of a considerable group of Dutch artists whose canvases prove the continued use in the churches of stained glass, painted organ shutters, and pulpits decorated with statuary.

Though not the only Dutch painter of the seventeenth century to occupy himself with Biblical themes, Rembrandt surpassed all others in depth of understanding and mastery of expression. The almost eight hundred and fifty designs in various media which he devoted to the Scriptures show the artist's steady growth as an interpreter of man's relation to the divine.

The youthful Rembrandt was mainly concerned with the dramatic aspects of the stories. Faces and gestures are marked by an overly intense emotionalism of excitement, anger, fear, or surprise. His color scheme was drab with extremes of chiaroscuro, the sharp contrast between light and dark areas derived ultimately from the works of Caravaggio. As Rembrandt matured he changed to a quieter, more introspective style. He had come to know suffering through the untimely death of his beloved wife and all their children except one son; he had learned what it means to be lonely and poor. His later work advanced from a portrayal of external action to a revelation of internal thought and feeling.

Comparing Rembrandt's early versions of *Abraham's Sacrifice,* the *Return of the Prodigal Son,* or the *Supper at Emmaus,* with those created at the height of his maturity is a most instructive experience. In each case almost violent action is stilled; what had come dangerously close to the theatrical has been changed into transparent sincerity. The Abraham of the early painting seems insensitive to the horror of the deed he has to perform and from which the angel barely holds him back. (PLATE 12) In the masterly late etching he is a grieving father on the brink of despair. His face is marked by the agony of the inner conflict through which he had to pass before he was ready to take the life of his only child. The late version of the *Return of the Prodigal Son,* one of the last paintings Rembrandt completed, is an unforgettable image of heartbroken repentance and infinitely grateful forgiveness, love meeting love in a fulfillment too deep for words. Thus Rembrandt must have hoped to be received home when his hour had come. The glowing red and gold tones, the luminous chiaroscuro have a warmth and an almost transcendental shimmer, reminding us of the beautiful word of George Fox, Rembrandt's contemporary in England: "I saw that there was an ocean of darkness and death, but an infinite ocean of Light and Love which flowed over the ocean of darkness."

To mention the founder of the Quaker movement in connection with Rembrandt is less farfetched than it may appear considering the artist's sympathies for the spiritually related Mennonite groups. Like the Quakers, they preached humility, love for one's neighbor, and peaceableness. Both were critical of churchly ceremony and ritual, chose lay ministers, and used silent prayer. "One gains the impression that the truly evangelical simplicity of the Mennonites, their sobriety, sincerity, and humility are reflected in Rembrandt's religious art much more than Calvinism, with its highly abstract and dialectic theology."[18] This view has been disputed, and Rembrandt's name is not on the membership lists of the Amsterdam Mennonite church. The Dutch theologian W. A. Visser 't Hooft has presented excerpts from Calvinist publications of the time to prove that Rembrandt could find support for his ideas in Calvinism as well. He rightly concluded: "Rembrandt's Christianity cannot be defined in terms of the church, but is the result of his personal encounter with the Bible." At first exploiting the Bible as a source for brilliant, though rather superficial compositions, he later "became the servant of the Word of God," letting it speak for itself without drawing attention to his technical skill.[19] Rembrandt confronted the glamour, self-assurance, and sense of triumph so evident in the baroque style with a faith born of suffering and love. (PLATE 13) He saw Christ in terms of Isaiah's words:

> He had no form or comeliness that we should look at him,
> and no beauty that we should desire him.
>
> (Isa. 53:2.)

Martin Luther and John Calvin had stressed the lowliness of Christ's humanity. Rembrandt followed them, yet he learned to give the features of the Savior something of the radiance that Peter must have apprehended when, in a moment of true inspiration, he exclaimed, "You are the Christ, the Son of the living God" (Matt. 16:16). This sense of the divine transfiguring the humble form of the preacher and teacher comes to us strongly from several of Rembrandt's portraits of Christ and the etching *Christ Preaching*. This modest work, still far too little known, brings us close to the Christ of the Gospels. Few artists before Rembrandt had ventured to represent Jesus preaching. The great difficulty of the task explains why this vital aspect of his ministry was almost passed by while numberless works of art glorify his Nativity and Passion. For unless the artist relies on the symbolism of a halo, he can convey a sense of Christ's presence only through the impact of his words and his whole being on those who hear him.

In Rembrandt's etching, men, women, and children have gathered in the back alley of an old city. Jesus talks slowly, with weighty gestures of his sensitive hands, and what he says has a personal meaning for each listener as different as their individual characters and experience of life. The portly man of wealth on Jesus' right is visibly perturbed by what he hears. His retainers lurk in the shadows behind him as if ready to lay their hands on the dreamer who scorns the rich and the mighty. A scholarly-looking man, a well-dressed traveler, a farmer or fisherman, weigh Jesus' words in their minds. Some old men on the far right are too tired, their souls too barren for the good seed to take root, and a dejected young man whose hunched shoulders indicate a disabling sickness, has not yet found the courage to believe and be healed. But the eyes of the crippled old beggar are widely open, as if, near the threshold of death, he saw the first glorious rays of an eternity of light.

As we read the faces of the people around Jesus, we suddenly find ourselves part of the group, irresistibly drawn into its circle by the gentleness, the human warmth, the utter sincerity of the humble, barefooted preacher. He must be Jesus, for no other prophet affected people in the same way, none spoke with as much love, even for the sinful and the lost. Might not the young woman seated at his feet and entirely absorbed in his message be one of these?

One has to study this etching to realize with what consummate skill Rembrandt has centered his composition unobtrusively around Jesus, bringing him close to the people and yet hinting at his loneliness. We marvel at Rembrandt's mastery of the human figure and its expressive qualities, at his ability to suggest much with a few significant lines. What inspiration could a good reproduction of this print bring to our church school children and their teachers, and to the members of the clergy! Ministers of the gospel surely ought to know Rembrandt well, not only for his interpretations of the Scriptures but also for the reason that no other artist has honored the

dignity and worth of the pastoral office as he did in his portrait of the Mennonite preacher Claesz Anslo consoling a grief-
stricken woman.

But by the middle of the seventeenth century the churches
of the Reformation had already settled in the rigid orthodoxy
that was so largely to dominate them. Rembrandt's freedom
from narrow dogmatism, his tolerance of other faiths (he
counted Catholics and Jews among his friends, besides the
sectarians), and his aversion to anything "pretty" or showy
caused his art to be neglected by official Protestant circles.
The spread of rationalism in the churches made his mystic approach appear outmoded. Rembrandt's emphasis on personal
experience of the faith — we may call it the "inner light" —
was not shared by minds intent on intellectual formalism.

Such minds found far greater appeal in the complex, often
abstruse sign language of the emblem, a combination of word
and image. It permitted almost infinite variation and lent itself
readily to learned speculation. Emblems became the great
rage during the period of rationalism when hundreds of "emblem books" were published. Beginning with the first major
collection of 1531, they became favorites especially of the Jesuits and other monastic orders. Their purpose was moralistic
and didactic: to illustrate a saying or epigram containing some
abstract truth either by visualizing it literally or by means of
parallels culled from nature, history, fable, or everyday life.
Emblems decorate ceilings, walls, altars, Bibles, collections of
sermons, children's books, catechisms, furniture, utensils, even
playing cards. Most of all, they flourished on tombs and monuments. Protestants were as enthusiastic about them as their
Catholic neighbors and calmly took over emblems originally
designed for the propagation of doctrines quite at variance
from their own.

The enormous popularity of the emblem lasted into the nineteenth century, as shown by a book published in Boston in
1846, with a second edition in 1855. It is entitled: *Religious
Emblems: Being a series of emblematic Engravings, with writ-*

ten explanations, miscellaneous observations and religious re-
flections, Designed to illustrate Divine Truth, in accordance
with the cardinal principles of Christianity. The authors were
William Holmes, minister of the gospel, and John W. Barber.
The engravings are amusingly quaint. An iceberg contrasted
with a rock stands for false principles against true ones. On a
pair of scales the Bible far outweighs a collection of books
marked "Fathers," "Councils," "Creeds," or simply ". . .
isms." "Selfishness" is exemplified by a foolish-looking man
burdened down by gold and silver, mortgages, tithes, deeds,
annuities, and so forth, barely stopping before a precipice
and heedless of the plight of a widow and her children in rags.
Each engraving is explained in a poem followed by several
pages of prose.

All this was well meant but reduces the great truths of the
faith to pious platitudes if not absurdities. The interest in emblems faded in the nineteenth century, though some live on in
the fraternal lodges and in the great seal of the United States.
One wonders how many Americans know the meaning of the
truncated pyramid with the eye above, surrounded by a radiance and the two inscriptions, *Annuit coeptis* and *Novus*
ordo seclorum, an emblem designed in 1776 and printed on
the back of every dollar bill.

The dryness of rationalism was answered by pietistic movements stressing an emotional religious experience. They, too,
tended to become involved in allegory — witness Bunyan's
The Pilgrim's Progress or Jacob Boehme's *Aurora* — and had no
eyes for the truly Protestant art of Rembrandt. To this day the
pietistically inclined prefer the lachrymose and oversweet style
of Guido Reni and his followers. Religious art (with the exception of architecture) sank to a low level during the later
seventeenth and eighteenth centuries and played an insignif-
icant role compared to religious poetry and music. No painter
or sculptor of this period can rank with Bach, Handel, Mozart,
or Beethoven.

Still, the people continued to express their faith in visual forms. Artisans in the Catholic regions, often with little or no technical schooling, produced considerable numbers of *santos* (images of saints), *retablos* (painted panels with a religious motive) and *bultos* (carvings). Their direct, primitive quality appeals greatly to the taste of our time. The nineteenth century, however, thought them crude and replaced them, like the old icons of the Greek Orthodox churches, with trite, conventional plaster "devotionals." Here and there popular religious art survived into the early years of our century in the form of the ex-votos, naïve representations of the helpful intervention of a saint or the Virgin Mary in moments of mortal danger, painted to fulfill a vow.

The folk arts of the Pennsylvania German (the so-called Dutch) offer an excellent example of how religious art motives persisted generation after generation among the members of a tradition-bound group. Their *Fraktur* technique of stylized calligraphy, illuminated with colorful ornaments, tulips, trees of life, and birds was used for baptismal and marriage certificates, rhymed *Haus-Segen* (home blessings), family records pasted into Bibles, and the like. Some show simply drawn figures: Adam and Eve in Paradise, angels, even the crucifixion. An example of 1847 shows the Roman soldiers still dressed in eighteenth-century uniforms, characteristic of the conservative outlook of folk artists. The flat, stylized treatment of the figures of Christ and the two thieves recalls early Irish manuscript illuminations of the eighth and ninth centuries. So does the intricate pattern of the *Fraktur,* reflecting the untrained artist's universal horror vacui, the fear of empty space.

The Pennsylvania Dutch also used sacred symbols for the decoration of chests, cupboards, butter molds, and other household utensils. Their cast-iron stove plates often show Biblical scenes done in low relief, usually with a Bible verse underneath. Such "folk" art had come with the settlers from their Palatinate homeland, where it was regularly practised, as it was in other parts of Germany and in Scandinavia. Swedish and Norwegian wall hangings of the eighteenth century frequently draw on Biblical motives such as the wise and foolish virgins, or the journey of the Magi, who are dressed in the fashionable costume of the time, complete with powdered queues. The Mennonites in America learned from their neighbors and did similar *Fraktur* sheets, generally embellished with the dove of peace and appropriate messages and appeals. The Shakers also occasionally produced designs of a related nature, the so-called inspirational drawings. (Shaker furniture is justly famed for its beautifully simple design.)

Religious themes remained fairly popular with the " Sunday painters " during the eighteenth and nineteenth centuries. The stories of the prodigal son and of the good Samaritan were occasionally told in sequence on separate canvases. The latter subject also appears on signboards, such as that preserved at the old pharmacy in Mystic seaport, Connecticut. Interestingly enough, scenes from the Old Testament were more numerous than those taken from the New, reflecting the persistent strong attachment to the revelation granted to the chosen people which had been part of the Puritan tradition.

Best known among these so-called Primitives are Erastus Field, painter of the delightful *Garden of Eden,* now in the Boston Museum of Fine Arts, and of other Scriptural subjects, and Edward Hicks, the inspired Quaker who never tired of repeating, always with slight variations, his favorite theme, the Peaceable Kingdom. It illustrates in a charming, childlike manner the prophecy of the Kingdom of God where " the wolf shall dwell with the lamb, and the leopard shall lie down with the kid, and the calf and the lion and the fatling together, and a little child shall lead them." Hicks followed the text very carefully and did not fail to include the sucking child playing over the hole of the asp, or the weaned child putting his hand on the adder's den. (Isa. 11:6-8.) The fervent Quaker often added in the background the scene of William Penn signing the peace treaty with the Indians. He saw in this act a perfect example of how Isaiah's words could be put into practice. (PLATE 14)

The scene was copied from a famous painting by an earlier Quaker artist, Benjamin West. America's first recognized great master of painting created a number of important religious compositions in the course of his long career, most of which was spent in Europe. West took his subjects from both the Old and the New Testaments. His *Raising of Lazarus,* painted for the Anglican Cathedral of Winchester, is now at Hartford, Connecticut; *Moses and the Brazen Serpent* was done for the Royal Chapel of Windsor Castle, *Christ Healing the Sick* was a gift of the artist, then president of the Royal Academy in London, to the Pennsylvania Hospital in Philadelphia. Like the huge canvas of *Death on a Pale Horse,* probably West's most famous work, they are large and ambitious efforts with many figures. When, in 1817, the painting *Christ Healing the Sick* was exhibited, the writer of a descriptive booklet showered it with praise. After discussing it in great detail he assures the reader: "America is possessed of a jewel, which, in later times, will attract to our shores men of taste and wealth from all other parts of the world."

G. From the Nineteenth Century to the Present

Alas, the prophecy did not come true. During West's lifetime, critics began to find fault with his bloodless, academic style and called the painting a failure. His many religious canvases are today well-nigh forgotten. He was too much the son of the age of enlightenment, too much the arranger and not enough the inspired creator, to infuse his work with the breath of life. His example, however, helped make Biblical themes acceptable to the American public. Copley, Trumbull, Washington Allston, Samuel F. B. Morse, and others followed suit. They were all handicapped by the prevailing fashion for "correct" drawing, which meant drawing either from posed models or, preferably, from prints after Raphael, Michelangelo, or casts of classical statuary. The religious paintings of these artists give the impression of intellectual and artistic exercises, not of the outgrowth of a compelling personal experience. Sometimes the painter left a project unfinished because he was aware of being inadequately equipped to master his ambitious theme. Allston almost despaired over his inability to complete the large composition of *Belshazzar's Feast* to his own satisfaction.

Similar difficulties plague the European artists of the time. The emphasis on line rather than on color gave little scope for forceful emotional expression. Perhaps only William Blake succeeded, though not always, in filling his linear designs with the ardor of a very personal faith. He had studied the writings of Swedenborg and, as a true mystic, often relied on visions for his inspiration. He was a man of few wants, happy with his dreams and sure of his message. The weaknesses of his drawing, and his lack of ability to give substance to the female figure, cannot overshadow his unique genius for rhythmic design. Unconcerned about models and working mainly from his boundless imagination, he combined memories of antiquity, the Gothic, and Michelangelo into his own characteristic style of flowing, swinging lines. Sometimes they explode like flashes of lightning as in some of the water colors on Revelation; at other times they move majestically, as in the *Third Temptation of Christ*, or the magnificent series to the story of Job. Soaring, triumphant lines make his *Ascension of Christ* one of the most inspired and inspiring versions of this difficult subject in Christian art. (PLATE 15)

Blake, like other artists, did not master the insuperable problem of envisaging God as Creator, but several of his designs approach Michelangelo's grandeur. The *Ancient of Days* shows a heroic figure reaching downward with a huge compass to give measure to chaos. In the water-color painting of *When the Morning Stars Sang Together*, one of Blake's finest, God is not the cosmic Power speaking to a terrified Job out of the whirlwind, but Wisdom and all-embracing Love, uniting heaven and earth in deepest concern for all. Ringed by stars, the beautiful sons of God truly shout for joy, and man can do no other than join their adoration. (PLATE 16)

Throughout Blake's work we sense the patent sincerity and radiant joy of a dedicated poet-artist who, shortly before his death, could say to a little girl: " May God make this world to you, my child, as beautiful as it has been to me." But Blake's romantic vision of love and brotherhood found no echo in his time. It was too personal and, like Rembrandt's, too independent of official doctrine and theology to be accepted by the churches. Not once was he asked to decorate the wall of a sanctuary or to paint an altarpiece. His works, for the most part the cherished treasures of our museums, are now at last beginning to speak to the Christian world.

A group of German painters of the same period met with greater acclaim. Young and enthusiastic, they rebelled against the iron rule of the art academies. In 1809 they founded the Brotherhood of St. Luke and settled in an empty convent in Rome. Theirs was a high idealism, strongly influenced by the reawakened admiration for the Middle Ages that was soon to lead to the Gothic Revival. The Nazarenes, as they were nicknamed on account of their religious piety, endeavored to recapture the clean, sharp, expressive line of the early German and Flemish painters as well as the spirituality they saw in the Italians and Raphael. Since the cold intellectualism of their own Lutheran Church offered nothing to them, most of the members of the group became converts to Roman Catholicism. Friedrich Overbeck, their leader, had been deeply impressed as a boy by some paintings in a Catholic chapel. They were poor adaptations of Italian Renaissance art, but they inspired him to follow the vocation of a religious painter. After studying the old masters he felt ready to re-create the sacred stories in a spirit of purity and beauty.

Neither Overbeck nor his friends had the artistic genius to accomplish what they intended to do. They lacked true originality and rarely advanced beyond clean, meticulously painted but inherently weak imitations of a style of the past. Their works undoubtedly have lyrical charm and grace, but there are no sharp edges in them; everything is too neatly ordered, too Sundaylike to stir up a vigorous response. Their Christ is an immaculate, gentle preacher always ready to forgive and to heal. The Danish sculptor Bertel Thorvaldsen, a friend of the Brotherhood, crystallized their image of the Savior in his statue of Christ, who, with open arms, invites " all who labor and are heavy-laden " to come to him. The beauty of Christ's regular features, his sad expression, the dignity of his figure enclosed in the melodious folds of a classic garment, have an immediate appeal. Yet prolonged reflection reveals the one-sidedness of the interpretation, for while it offers consolation of those " who are heavy-laden," it is difficult to find in it in-spiration for those " who labor." Thorvaldsen, like the Naz-arenes, gave no hint of Christ's inner strength, his grasp of the realities of life. To see in the Savior only the bearer of our burdens and not also the leader who demands of us sacrificial love is to fall short of the whole truth of the gospel. This failure to penetrate to the core of the Christian message stymied the efforts of the Nazarenes. What they had hopefully planned as a new beginning turned out to be a retreat.

Precisely, this backward-looking, unworldly character of the art of the Nazarenes and their imitators assured it of wide ac-ceptance at a time when people looked upon religion as a refuge from the harshness of their ever-more complex and competitive daily life. They fled into sentimentality because the Christian faith as then preached by the churches had lost the strength or the will to challenge the social order, and yielded the vital center of civilization to philosophy, politics, economics, and, increasingly, science and technology. In the older nations of Europe the churches allied themselves with the ruling classes on whose support they largely depended, and abandoned their role as the conscience of society. The churches made little or no effort to understand the justified outcries of the exploited laboring classes and left them to drift into indifference or hostility toward the Christian faith.

Out of touch with the creative forces of their epoch, the churches, for the first time in Christian history, were incapable of stimulating the arts. Their buildings imitated Greek temples or Gothic cathedrals; their paintings, statuary, and decorative elements were equally backward-looking, with copies of Italian Renaissance masters greatly in demand. A faith without real power and substance was mirrored in the well-intentioned but spineless compositions of artists who would long since have been forgotten had the churches not chosen them as their flag-bearers: Hofmann, Schmalz, Plockhorst, Portaels, Calderon, and numerous others. Gérôme and Munkácsy, technically well trained, cover large canvases with pseudohistorical spectacles in tedious exactness of detail. Bouguereau produced stilted, emotion-oozing religious paintings and, at the same time, though for a different clientele, some of the most sensuous studio nudes.

With complete unconcern about the artist's affiliation, Protestant, Catholic, and Orthodox churches alike accepted this feeble ersatz art. In America it became the heyday of the chromo, and commercial interests were not slow to discover a gold mine in the popularization of this type of religious art. Reproductions are still seen in churches and Sunday school rooms, serve as models for church pageants and Hollywood movies, and supply the core of the "devotionals" at the dime stores.

The American churches had started out on a different note. The severely simple wooden meetinghouses of the New England settlers were perfectly adapted to the harsh conditions of life in a sparsely inhabited, heavily wooded country. Lack of skilled craftsmen and Puritan abhorrence of elaboration kept decoration at a minimum. As the sermon was the center of the worship service, a squarish plan, with pews arranged along three sides facing the raised pulpit and the Communion table, was preferred. These buildings have "style" because they are the consistent expression of the religious views of the settlers. They communicate as little of the joy Christ promised his _____ as does the stern Puritan faith, but when we enter sympathetically into their spirit we can appreciate their quiet, austere beauty.

By the eighteenth century the extreme rigor of Puritanism had faded. With increasing wealth and comfort, the thinking of the colonists assumed some of the urbanity of contemporary Britain. Church design gained in attractiveness; a sophisticated charm overlaid the rugged, homespun simplicity of the earlier structures. Many buildings of this period and of the early decades of the nineteenth century are unusually appealing. Yet the danger signs of a spiritual ebb tide are already apparent in this very gentility. Elegant proportions and details betray a desire to conform, to be " of " the world rather than merely " in " it. The church no longer shaped society in its image. On the contrary, an enlightened society captured the church and impressed on it its outlook and taste.

The separation of church and state encouraged the growth of independent denominations in America, greatly varying in creedal emphasis and form of organization. Competing with one another, they paid more attention to theological differences than to their paramount task of confronting society with the vital message of Christ. Spiritual stagnation was bound to set in.

The vast expansion of population, the growth of the cities, and the settlement of the West necessitated a huge building program that left little to spare for works of painting and sculpture. Native artists had a difficult time getting proper training, since the country had a paucity of museums and art schools. Interest in the creative arts had not yet progressed to the point where painters could earn a living, except those who specialized in portraiture, until the Hudson River school made landscape popular. Thomas Cole, the leader of this group of artists, was also sincerely interested in religious subjects. He kept a Bible open in his studio while painting his elaborate allegorical canvases *Life, Death, and Immortality* and *The Cross and the World*. His approach, similar to that of the Nazarenes, was too sermonizing, however, to result in convincing works. This is also true of William Page, the American Titian. Neither of them received a single commission or even encouragement from the churches at a time when copies after old masters and feeble examples of post-Nazarene religious art crossed the Atlantic in large numbers.

A new promise appeared around the middle of the century in England. William Holman-Hunt, John Everett Millais, Dante Gabriel Rossetti, and their friends of the Pre-Raphaelite Brotherhood revolted against the routine of the academies and the soulless, conventional style they fostered. They aimed at perfect truth through the careful study and delineation of minute detail. Inspired by lofty ideals, they chose some of the noblest subjects of religion and poetry and made the masters of the early Renaissance — Fra Angelico, Botticelli, and the Flemish painters — their heroes rather than Raphael, thereby scandalizing a public used to seeing in Raphael the highest perfection of the art of painting. Though short-lived (1848–1853), the Brotherhood exerted considerable influence. Thanks mainly to the support of John Ruskin, they gradually found wide approval. Paintings such as Holman-Hunt's *Light of the World,* Millais' *Christ in the Carpenter's Shop,* and Ford Madox Brown's *Christ Washing St. Peter's Feet* have since become widely known and still command respect.

But once more the hopes their first efforts had awakened were to be disappointed. Their style hardened, sentimentality crept in, along with a desire for effects. The Pre-Raphaelite movement was in the end doomed to fail because its orientation was to the past, not the future. Some of the early works of these artists are sincere and original in concept, but most of what they did later appears today dated, definitely Victorian. Their ideal of beauty proved to be artificial and nostalgic and did not reflect the great forces then shaping Western civilization.

Besides, even these idealistically minded artists were subconsciously influenced by the materialistic outlook of their time. It comes to the fore in their overly detailed technique and their obsession with supposedly historical setting and costumes. Holman-Hunt traveled to the Holy Land in search of local color for his Biblical scenes, something artists had never thought necessary or desirable in the past, and was followed by others. They blithely assumed that the Arab population of Palestine, then an impoverished and backward country, had remained close to Biblical times in dress and way of life. As a consequence of this misconception, scores of paintings and illustrations from the late nineteenth century on show the Biblical scenes in purely Arab surroundings, and the idea has firmly entrenched itself in the minds of many Christians.

In the meantime, French painters gave proof that the timeless stories of the Bible could still inspire artists of true creative vision. Eugène Delacroix rendered incidents from the Old Testament and the life and Passion of Christ with dramatic power. His *Christ in the Storm,* several versions of which are in American museums, is one of the most impressive visualizations of the story; the *Agony in the Garden* is the more moving because it shows a strong, virile Christ. Edouard Manet's occasional religious subjects are courageous but isolated attempts to apply the naturalistic style to familiar themes and thereby bring them closer to our time. Courbet's *Funeral at Ornans* handles an everyday motive of religious overtones with the objectivity of a journalistic report and achieves a dignity comparable to the cemetery scene in Thornton Wilder's play *Our Town.* Honoré Daumier's *Ecce Homo* treats the scene as if it were contemporary. The bold and dramatic painting, far too little known, makes us regret that the great painter never received the slightest encouragement from the churches.

These artists opposed the correctness and storytelling literalness then demanded, but it took the long struggle of the Impressionists to break the power of the guardians of a dead past and give art a new vitality. Their preoccupation, however, was with nature — with sunlight, air, and the living, breathing human figure. Absorbed in the vibrant beauty of the world, they showed no interest in religious themes. The age-old link between art and faith was broken because a stagnant church turned its back to the creative forces of its time. If art and faith were to join again to their mutual blessing, the churches would have to wake up to their responsibility to the culture of their time.

Signs of such an awakening began to appear in the second half of the century. Thoughtful churchmen could not remain silent in the face of the evils of a dog-eat-dog economy and the unrest and spiritual homelessness of the workers. The "Social Gospel" proclaimed Christian concern for the community against the excesses of unbridled individualism. Gladden, Rauschenbusch, and others recognized that Christ's message of salvation applied to the social order as well as to the person. Where human beings are treated as means to an end, the command of brotherly love is violated and the Kingdom of God betrayed.

It was as if Christian art had been waiting for such a renewal. Was it mere coincidence that the Pre-Raphaelite Brotherhood was founded in the same year that saw the beginning of the Christian Socialist movement in England under the leadership of Maurice and Kingsley? When Wichern and Harnack threw German Lutheranism into uproar, Eduard von Gebhardt and Fritz von Uhde added fuel to the fire with their new religious art. Gebhardt ventured only halfway, so to speak, by using the Reformation period as the setting for his scenes from the life of Christ, not his own time. Uhde went all the way and boldly placed a humble, unglamorous Savior in a country school where the children are meeting him in a completely delightful, natural way, or in a green Tyrolean meadow where farmers and farm women reverently listen to his words.

Lhermitte in France tried to do very much the same. Eugène Carrière sometimes achieved moving effects with his shadowy, indistinct figures. His *Christ on the Cross* in the Louvre has strength and simplicity of design. Maurice Denis made a valuable contribution to the regeneration of religious art by combining the bright colors of the Impressionists with Cézanne's and Gauguin's sense for abstract form qualities. The carefully organized patterns, especially of his murals, have dignity and helped prepare the ground for some of the best contemporary work. Denis was a devout Roman Catholic. When he placed Christ in surroundings of our time he applied to art the spirit of the encyclical *Rerum novarum* of 1891 in which Pope Leo XIII discussed social and economic problems much as the leaders of the Protestant " Social Gospel " were doing. Denis liked to give his paintings a calm, serene air inviting meditation, but it often hides his message behind a veil of aloofness.

The opposite is true of Vincent van Gogh. His whole outlook on life was deeply religious. He tried literally to live the " Social Gospel " in the poor mining district of the Borinage in Belgium before finding in painting the outlet he needed for his urge for community. The memory of his difficulties with church officials perhaps kept him from attempting religious compositions of his own, for his rare Biblical paintings are free variations of Rembrandt and Delacroix, enhanced by his almost violent energy in brushwork and color. In *The Raising of Lazarus* he singled out a group from Rembrandt's large etching of 1632, omitting Christ as if he felt inadequate to do him justice. We see only the moment when the miracle reveals itself to Mary and Martha. With excited gestures, as much terrified as relieved, they watch their dead brother wake again in the tomb. Every line, every dab of color, shouts and swirls in this ecstatic work and draws us irresistibly into its emotional force. (PLATE 17) Vincent van Gogh's paintings of flowers and landscapes speak with the same religious fervor. " He expresses the sigh of the creation in his Provence scenes where trees twist, the sun circles, the earth lifts itself up like those hills of which the psalmist says that they ' skip like lambs ' " (Ps. 114:4).[20]

Van Gogh's directness of expression swept away traditional

ideas of religious art and opened the door for the vital new Christian painting and sculpture of our time. It also helped us to rediscover the long-forgotten genius of El Greco. The Spanish mystic's work is aflame with a similar sense of urgency, resembling Van Gogh's in the free use of distortion for the sake of emotional emphasis. But Van Gogh died in despair over the ridicule and contempt heaped upon him. He had sold only a single painting of the hundreds in which he had poured out his love for all creation. Now they are universally admired and sell for almost unbelievable sums.

The torch he had carried passed into the hands of others, equally intent on the absolute truth of religious experience and unafraid of shocking the complacent and the conformists. French painters of the Fauve group, most consistently Georges Rouault, the Belgian Emile Raes, and the German Expressionists — Nolde, Beckmann, Nauen, Heckel, the great sculptor Ernst Barlach, Käthe Kollwitz — felt strongly the glaring contrast between the teachings of Christ and the unconcerned materialism of a civilization drifting ever closer to a world war. Purposely choosing strident colors and violently distorted forms, they created stirring works sometimes reminiscent of Grünewald, who was likewise rediscovered at this time. (PLATE 18)

José Clemente Orozco's angry Christ, at Dartmouth College; Graham Sutherland's *Crucifixion,* at Northampton, England; the American Rico Lebrun's terrifying version of this theme and his Buchenwald paintings; Umberto Romano's *Ecce Homo* — all are spiritual descendants of the Isenheim Altar. They are meant to disturb, to rouse the sleeping conscience of the Christian world. (PLATES 19, 20) The early work of Georges Rouault, whom critics have called the greatest religious artist of the twentieth century, is like a despairing outcry against the ugliness and corruption he saw around him, unrelieved by a ray of hope. Gradually his bitter scorn changed into deep compassion for all suffering. To study the monumental prints of his series *Miserere* and *Guerre* is a moving experience. (They are now available, though reduced in size, in a publication of The Museum of Modern Art, New York.) He takes us to the chambers where the dying call out from the depths, to Calvary and a Christ who " will be in agony until the end of the world " but who is also " obedient unto death, even death on a cross " (Phil. 2:8). One of the most impressive plates, entitled *Sometimes the Blind Have Comforted Those Who See,* is a profound symbol of man's need for brotherhood. (PLATE 21)

The parallels between the vision of these artists and the insights of the new theology of crisis are striking. Barth, Tillich, Brunner, Berdyaev, and others may differ in their views, but they share with the best Christian artists of our age the conviction that man is unable to save himself unaided, that he depends utterly on God. The spokesmen of the churches have confessed to the tragic failure of the churches to stand up against naked evil. The Christian faith reached a new dimension of depth when Bishop Hanns Lilje, one of the leaders of the Confessing Church in Germany, could write out of his own sufferings in a concentration camp: " At this extreme limit of human life it becomes clear why God is with those who are despised, outcast, tortured, imprisoned, disinherited, and solitary. . . . Man's situation is such that God *can* only have mercy upon him. . . . Man can only really exist at all because God has declared him, a sinner, to be justified, because he promises him, who is under the power of death, eternal life." [21]

This is what contemporary Christian artists proclaim. They refuse to paint a rosy, optimistic picture of life and of man. With almost ruthless disregard for outward beauty they speak the truth that alone can lead us to God's mercy. In these days when the world trembles on the brink of nuclear catastrophe it would be a denial of the reality of our situation to show a Christ without the tragic implication of the cross.

Yet already some of the younger artists here and abroad are

beginning to proclaim a renewed faith in God's unshaken love
and the redemption even of our world through Jesus Christ.
They are reaching for the more mature wisdom that William
Law expressed when he wrote: "Men are not in hell because
God is angry with them; they are in wrath and darkness because they have done to the light, which infinitely flows forth
from God, as that man does to the light of the sun, who puts
out his own eyes." We can observe these stirrings of a vital
new Christian art in our own country and particularly in
Europe. Great exhibitions have given proof of the astonishing
scope and richness of work in every medium being done in
many places by dedicated artists. (PLATE 22) Almost every
issue of the American Roman Catholic quarterly *Liturgical Arts*
and of various French, German, and Italian journals of Christian art present new evidence.

Sculpture seems to be leading the way. The impressive work
of Bourdelle, Sir John Epstein, Mestrovic, Marcks, and Manzù,
Henry Moore's great Madonna at Northampton, England, and
a group of new bronze doors for churches and cathedrals in
Austria and Germany demonstrate the power of contemporary
artists to state the timeless truth of the faith in new forms.
Heinz Warneke, Henry Kreis, and Charles Umlauf are among
the sculptors of outstanding significance in our own country.
Umlauf's *Pieta*, the *Crucifixus* at St. Mark's Church in Burling-
ton, Vermont, *Christ and the Children*, and other statues combine depth of feeling and disciplined, expressive form. His
figure *Man Facing Eternity* is a moving symbol of modern
man's search for the light of faith. (PLATE 23)

Perhaps the most encouraging sign of new life is the sudden
emergence of an authentic modern church architecture. Louis
Sullivan's dynamic expression, "Form follows function," became the key that liberated builders caught in the prison of
a historical orientation. The influence of his pupil, Frank Lloyd
Wright, encouraged new ventures first in Europe, then in this
country, and was largely responsible for the rapid spread of
modern "functional" design.

New materials and methods of construction were at first almost shamefacedly hidden behind the old, borrowed forms. This illogical procedure disappeared after Frank Lloyd Wright had shown its lack of logic and honesty. Perret's church in Le Raincy, France, built in 1923, was the first to utilize the possibilities of concrete without any attempt at disguise. Both here and in a church at St. Denis, Perret created interiors of a clarity that disarmed his critics. Moser and Metzger in Switzerland and Bohm in Germany made further advances. It took years to work out the problems involved, and for a while the pendulum swung too strongly in the direction of starkness unrelieved by grace. Not so much the leaders as some of their more doctrinaire followers were casting aside the valid strength of tradition together with its sham and pretense. The urgent need to build quickly a large number of European churches destroyed in World War II, and the accelerated American population shift from the cities into the suburbs, set into motion a wave of church construction abroad and here that has not yet abated. Architects were now prepared for the task. Men like Bartning, Schwarz, Novarina, Le Corbusier, Niemeyer, Saarinen, Belluschi, and many others achieved impressive and challenging new solutions. Daring structures such as the hill chapel at Ronchamp near Belfort, France, the First Presbyterian Church of Stamford, Connecticut, and the chapel of the Massachusetts Institute of Technology in Cambridge, Massachusetts, have already become world-famous.

The last few years have seen bold new departures from accustomed patterns. Churches using the steeply rising tent shape or the parabola, with entirely new seating plans, unusual bell towers, and new forms of stained glass set into concrete have risen in Mexico, Brazil, Italy, Spain, Poland, Holland, the United States, and other countries as well. All the major Christian denominations are sharing in the search, some enthusiastically, others more hesitantly. There is, of course, a great deal of poorly considered routine building still going on, and many congregations lack the courage of conviction. But the new churches and the new works of Christian art are gaining friends because they speak to the people of our time in a language instinctively felt as our own. Indeed, what we are witnessing today, almost as if by a miracle, is a new encounter between art and the Christian faith.

Chapter III

The Function of Christian Art

> *It is a serious error to take conventionalism for a kind of humility. God will not stand for any kind of lukewarmness. He demands silence or boldness.*
> — Jean Cocteau.

A. Art and the Corporate Worship of the Church

For nearly eighteen hundred years art has accompanied the Christian faith as it passed from one generation to another. Unlike books gathering dust on library shelves, it is before the eyes of the people as part of their world. Regardless of the wishes of any particular group, religious art and imagery are given facts in a pluralistic society and cannot be ignored. Any church alive to the conditions under which it proclaims its message to our time will have to consider the problems involved. One wonders if all our churches realize how deeply visual impressions can influence religious concepts and attitudes. A worshipful, clean, well-cared-for church building speaks of the congregation's high regard for the life of faith. A cold, neglected church can evoke a sense of fear, indifference, even hostility. A religious picture on a wall calendar may shape a child's mental image of Christ long before he has learned anything definite about the Christian faith.

The major difficulty lies in the lack of an adequate theology of Christian art for our time, both among the nonliturgical and the liturgical churches, the latter of which have traditionally been friendly to the visual arts. The fear of idolatry that led to bitter strife in the past is, fortunately, no longer a matter of real concern. Christian churches are unanimous in condemning the adoration of images. Predominantly illiterate populations doubtless still confuse adoration and veneration, the latter being permitted in Catholic and Orthodox practice. But where both clergy and people are fully literate, the distinction is clearly understood. Only the uninformed — or prejudiced — can claim that any Christian church permits the worship of paintings or statues. "In fact, today, there is much greater danger of bibliolatry than of idolatry in the ordinary sense of the word, particularly amongst those to whom visual imagery has no immediate appeal."[1]

However, opinions about the use of religious art differ widely with the various denominations, and from one local congregation to the next. These different viewpoints have prevented the formulation of generally acceptable principles and limit the validity of statements on the relation between the church and the arts. There is considerable agreement on the value of the visual approach as an aid in instruction and for the devotional life of the individual, but far less in connection with the worship services of the church. In one of his " Choruses from ' The Rock,'" T. S. Eliot has succinctly expressed the case for the arts:

> Lord, shall we not bring these gifts to Your service?
> Shall we not bring to Your service all our powers
> For life, for dignity, grace and order,
> And intellectual pleasures of the senses?
> The Lord who created must wish us to create
> And employ our creation again in His service
> Which is already His service in creating.
> For Man is joined spirit and body,
> And therefore must serve as spirit and body.[2]

Unfortunately, the church has sometimes been guilty of an overemphasis on externals that led to sharp reactions against ritual, the arts, even music as distracting and super-

fluous. When such hostility took the extreme form of iconoclasm, Christian life usually dried up in a joyless, often enough
loveless, routine. Neither stern rigor nor overelaborate formalism ought to stifle the direct, spontaneous communion of the
soul with God.

Some of the opposition against ritual and the use of the
arts as aids in worship is based on the idea that nothing
matters except the proclamation of the gospel. Indeed, the
first task of the church is always to preach the good news of
salvation to a despairing world in terms of its own experience
and understanding. A market place, street corner, clearing in
the woods, or any other place where people gather can serve
the purpose. It did so in the time of Jesus and the apostles and
still does where missionary work is the primary requisite. A
tent or empty store is sufficient to give shelter from heat, rain,
and snow.

Yet once the church is established it demands more than
a temporary meeting place. Men and women who have become
followers of Christ no longer walk alone; confessing their
faith in the same leader, they are drawn together into a community. So, after Christ's ascension, were the disciples when
they came back to the upper room and "with one accord
devoted themselves to prayer" (Acts 1:14). From Pentecost
on, they were the church, the living body of Christ. They discovered that faith is realized in its fullest measure only through
common worship. Jesus said, "Where two or three are gathered in my name, there am I in the midst of them." (Matt.
18:20.)

Brotherly love cannot become effective without community.
It needs the soil of the church to grow and be sustained.
"Corporate and personal worship . . . should complete, re-
inforce, and check each other. Only where this happens . . .
do we find in its perfection the normal and balanced life of
full Christian devotion." [3]

The heart of Christian worship is adoration. It is man's
answer to the compelling sense of awe that comes to him from

the recognition of how infinitely God transcends the farthest reaches of our thoughts. As we join with others in adoration, we leave behind the narrow confines of the self and open our souls to God as the ground of all being. Adoration leads to praise and thanksgiving, not because God needs such tokens but because we do. Worship remains barren without praise, "that is, the fruit of lips that acknowledge his name" (Heb. 13:15). The Te Deum Laudamus of the church lifts into the consciousness of each worshiper his absolute dependence on the Creator, who "holds the whole world in his hands." Awesome distance remains between God and man, but through God's self-revelation in the history of the "chosen people" and in Jesus Christ a fellowship is made possible that is both joy and challenge.

This is the great paradox of the incarnation: "God was in Christ reconciling the world to himself" (II Cor. 5:19). Through Christ, we are no longer "strangers and sojourners, but . . . fellow citizens with the saints and members of the household of God, built upon the foundation of the apostles and prophets, Christ Jesus himself being the chief cornerstone, in whom the whole structure is joined together and grows into a holy temple in the Lord" (Eph. 2:19-21). Paul here states allegorically what the church has to put into visible form. A camp-meeting site or gospel tent are too temporary in character to satisfy for long the needs of the community of believers. The household of God must have an enduring house for its worship: to gather around the Lord's Table, to hear the gospel proclaimed and interpreted, and to develop a living sense of unity. It is also needed for teaching the faith, for Baptism and the solemnization of marriage vows, and for the burial service for the dead.

Music, poetry, and the visual arts have no higher function in the Christian life than to enter into the service of God by becoming part of the corporate worship of the church. The dedication to God of all that is best in man is his only acceptable answer to God's boundless love manifested in Jesus

Christ and in the gift of the Holy Spirit. The great concept of the priesthood of all believers does not imply that all should be preachers or leaders. Any act of selfless devotion becomes a priestly act, be it teaching in the church school, working on a church committee, preparing food for a group meeting, or cleaning the building. These and other ways of serving are rightly considered worthy offerings in the spirit of Paul's explicit instructions. (Rom. 2:6-8; I Cor. 12:4-11; Eph. 4:11-12.) We also accept as valid Christian service the writing and composing of hymns and other religious music, and the ministry of organist and choir.

Should, then, the creative gifts of the architect, sculptor, painter, and craftsman be withheld from the self-offering of the community to God? The Gospels consistently stress the surpassing value of the sense of sight. Christ said: " Your eye is the lamp of your body; when your eye is sound, your whole body is full of light." (Luke 11:34.) Through the language of the eye, art can help the believing community to fulfill Paul's exhortation to " be filled with the Spirit," to sing and make melody to the Lord, and to give " thanks in the name of our Lord Jesus Christ to God the Father " (Eph. 5:18-20).

B. The House of God

The first and foremost task of the arts, then, is to provide a suitable setting for the corporate worship of the church. The instant we plan to build more than the simplest kind of shelter, design, the basic characteristic of all art, has to enter. The only question, therefore, is whether the design is good, bad, or indifferent. The answer depends far less on decorative forms than on the clear expression of the purpose and function of the whole structure.

We know from our own experience in workshop or office, school or hospital, how a well-designed environment can make life and work more productive and satisfying. The same holds true of the home, except that ideally it should also reflect something of our personality, our ideals, and our outlook on life, in order to become more than merely a place in which to live.

A congregation that is truly alive has a distinct personality of its own. It will feel most deeply "at home" in a church building that embodies its particular spirit of faith and worship. Neither a ready-made design nor the most accurate imitation of a style of the past can do that. This is not to deny the value of tradition. Worship in a centuries-old church enriches us by making us aware of continuity. We see ourselves as a link in a chain binding the past to the present and, we hope, the future. The faith of our fathers is almost visibly enshrined in a time-hallowed church and enfolds us in its assurance. Gratitude to those who labored to raise this house of God can inspire us to do our share of work for the Kingdom. Yet there is always a subtle temptation to rest on the achievements of the fathers, to idolize the past. Pride in a tradition to which we have not made our own positive contribution can lead to a snobbish, condescending attitude and a more or less openly declared exclusiveness. Such a church may perhaps be the first in social standing but will scarcely be first in the eyes of the Savior. Time and again he warned us that to be granted privileges places on us a greater obligation to serve our less fortunate neighbors.

The problem of tradition has an entirely different aspect when a new church is to be built. The very first step ought always to be a thorough self-examination on the part of the congregation. Does it hold the truths of the faith as they were stated long ago to be fully equal to the needs of the present age? Does it wish to emphasize its connection with the historic roots of Christianity, or with earlier stages in the growth of its own denomination? Have creed and ritual remained substantially unchanged? If this is so, the choice of a traditional design can be defended as logical and sincere. Otherwise, it merely betrays a desire to stay safely within the commonly accepted pattern of respectability and general appeal. For a young congregation in a brand-new development or in an industrial area to give itself the appearance of antiquity would amount to pretense.

If, on the other hand, a congregation believes that the insights and formulations of the faith are changing as God reveals his will to men through the continuous working of the Holy Spirit; if it holds it to be essential for the church to confront its own age with a prophetic voice challenging evil and sin; if it is actively engaged in evangelism and missions, and concerned with all the urgent problems of contemporary society, it will be right in choosing a contemporary design.

Some acid comments, some sharp criticism, can be expected. But such initial antagonism will quickly fade if the building and its furnishings are truly well designed to express the inner motivation of the church family. While those to whom the " good old days " are forever dear may remain lukewarm in their approval, the men, women, and young people whose minds are attuned to our age will respond to the appeal of new forms with enthusiasm. Experience has shown that courageous new designs excite admiration and attract many who were indifferent or had become estranged from the faith, perhaps in the belief that it had no vital message for them. The Evangelical Church in Bavaria, for instance, has found that attendance at services has greatly increased in newly built, modern churches. In Hamburg it has doubled and in some cases tripled. Similar observations were made in France, where it was also noted that working-class congregations took very readily to churches designed in contemporary forms.

Critics of recent trends frequently object to experiments in church architecture. They believe that earlier styles, especially the Gothic, are fully adequate and satisfying and, moreover, immediately identify a church. Actually, this is not the case. Libraries, town halls, schools and colleges, private dwellings, even penitentiaries, constructed within the last hundred years have utilized the same forms. Early skyscrapers, too, were dressed up in " Gothic." Every new venture entails a risk of failure, and not all modern churches will stand the test of time. For this, the past offers plentiful parallels. A new style does not spring full-grown into existence but has to pass through a stage of trial and error. Besides, architects differ in their abilities. Some are original and inventive creators; others merely adapt themselves to prevailing trends. We are still too close to the beginnings of the new "functional" style in contemporary architecture to evaluate it objectively, but it has already produced enough inspiring church buildings to be considered a valid expression of faith for our age.

Nothing in the Christian faith recommends taking the safe and easy way. It began with a revolutionary protest against traditions and institutions of long standing. Today, as of old, it demands the courage of conviction. To follow Jesus is to be ready for changes, be it in the life of the individual or of the community. Building in one of the historic styles may avoid aesthetic pitfalls and dangers, but praise and thanksgiving to God are most sincere when spoken in our own language. Our task, as the eminent German church architect Rudolf Schwarz sees it, is "to build churches out of that reality which we experience and verify every day; to take this our own reality so seriously and to recognize it to be so holy that it may be able to enter in before God. . . . The substance of all church building, its own meaning, sacred, irreplaceable and inexchangeable, is the living church." [4]

Such thinking motivates the Christian artists and architects of our time in their search for new forms. Materials and methods of construction available today offer possibilities far beyond the dreams of former generations. Problems of spatial design once considered insoluble can now be mastered. There is, for example, no longer a structural necessity to use interior supports such as columns and piers, or heavy walls of masonry, buttresses, and pinnacles. Wide rooms made possible through the use of structural steel, reinforced concrete, laminated wood, or glass can unite the congregation in clear, uncluttered spaces. A dramatic flow of light, sometimes achieved through deeply recessed windows, can focus the eyes of the worshipers on altar or pulpit.

Examples of contemporary church architecture are of an almost bewildering variety of forms. They have enough in common, however, aside from the imaginative use of new techniques, to reveal dominant characteristics in keeping with the highest ideals of the faith. Foremost among them is a resolute insistence on honesty, sometimes carried to the point where the structural skeleton remains fully visible in walls or ceiling. The materials used are permitted to speak for themselves, without surface veneers. Every part of the church building is to be truthful because we are under the command to worship God in spirit and in truth. We no longer hide brick under a plaster covering treated to resemble marble as was done even in St. Peter's in Rome, much to the distress of the observant visitor. Such honesty, often resulting in a simplicity reminiscent of Franciscan or Puritan churches, presents the church in "nakedness before God" and asks us likewise to come to him in utmost sincerity, for he is not deceived. This austerity is sometimes felt as harsh and uninviting because we are still accustomed to the richly decorated church interiors of the past.

Yet this poverty in Christ need not be dispirited. Subtle handling of textures and lively, unexpected forms banish the impression of monotony without making concessions to a desire for "catchy" effects. Careful adjustments of the relations between height, width, and length, and precise planning of every detail in harmony with the whole, can give the church dignity without stuffiness in an atmosphere conducive to prayer and meditation.

From the coherent planning of the entire church its main front or façade then arises in logical conclusion. Sometimes it has been turned into a wall of glass to stress the "openness" of the church, though care must be taken lest the worshiping congregation be distracted by what is passing on the outside. The main point is that the exterior of a good contemporary church is not arbitrarily chosen and, so to speak, added for the sake of decoration or show, an impression we get from not a few routine buildings of earlier times. Modern exteriors are worked out as a summation of what the whole building wants to say to the community of the spiritual life of the congregation. They shun the commonplace and the innocuous. They desire to awaken sleepy souls and ask for commitment, for a yes or no. Their builders are not afraid of criticism. What matters to them is that the church should proclaim its message to an age dominated by materialistic concerns "not in plausible words of wisdom, but in demonstration of the Spirit and power" (I Cor. 2:4).

Two aspects of corporate worship which, more than others, have suffered from lack of sensitivity for the relation between the spiritual life and the visual arts are the baptismal and the funeral service. The former presents special problems due to the widely varying views regarding immersion, dipping, or sprinkling, and infant versus adult Baptism. The entire theology of Baptism may be said to be in flux. But until we have achieved greater unanimity, we could still enhance the rite by providing for it a more appealing spatial setting, whether near the entrance (because Baptism is the gate through which we come into the church of Christ), or near the altar (as a symbol of our dedication of ourselves and our children to a life of Christian service). The font, nowadays often so small that it has been compared to a birdbath, deserves more attention than it has customarily received. In a good modern church the architect will either design it himself or entrust it to a sculptor. In view of the fact that nearly all denominations consider Baptism to be one of the sacraments, it is surprising how few really beautiful fonts can be seen in American Protestant churches, and how rarely our sculptors have been given the opportunity to make Baptism more meaningful through their art. Yet some of the medieval bronze and stone baptismal fonts belong to the great masterpieces of sculpture, and contemporary examples by outstanding artists worthily continue this tradition.

When the churches permitted the funeral service to become the domain of the undertaker, they gave up the right to influence its setting. The consequences are deplorable. Anyone who has conducted such a service from a lectern in a hallway, with the family and friends of the deceased out of sight to the right and left, will have experienced embarrassment, if not shame. The fault lies not with the funeral directors who generally try hard to make their places neat and attractive. But their " parlors " were usually built as residences and cannot easily be changed. They breathe an impersonal air of gentility and efficiency. Inoffensive color prints of still-life paintings or landscapes adorn the walls; soft carpets hush the sound of footsteps. Under the given conditions one can scarcely ask for more from what are essentially business establishments.

But we could have something entirely different and decidedly more Christian in character. As an act of corporate worship the funeral service has its rightful place in the church or a special chapel at the cemetery. Several recently built mortuary chapels of this kind in Europe show a quiet beauty and dignity that cannot fail to console and lift up grief-stricken hearts. A mosaic or sculpture symbolic of the resurrection proclaims the Christian faith in the life eternal. The atmosphere is neither lugubrious nor casual, as it so often is in the " funeral home." It speaks of trust and joy even under tears, of the hope that our faith in the Savior affirms. Such chapels are still rare in our country. They could be built if local churches were willing to work together.

At the same time, the churches might take steps to improve the appearance of the cemeteries, some of which are among the worst eyesores in our communities. It was not so in the early centuries when simplicity and a large degree of uniformity prevailed, suggesting that wealth and position count for nothing before God. Some denominations, like the Friends and the Mennonites, still adhere to this concept, but the majority succumbed to the fashion for more and more elaborate grave monuments, a fashion that began to spread in the early nineteenth century, perhaps influenced by the Italian *campo santos*. Urns, obelisks, whole or broken columns, and statuary of all descriptions proliferated, but very rarely the work of trained sculptors. The failure of the churches to give direction and counsel must bear a large share of responsibility for the inexcusable travesty of the faith represented by some cemeteries. The time is ripe for a new approach to the problem. Much could be done if the National Council of Churches, with the active co-operation of landscape architects, artists, and makers of memorials, established over-all principles and showed how these could be translated into practice. Once the churches are ready to call on the services of the artists of our time, a solution can be found. Käthe Kollwitz' deeply moving tombstone design *Rest in the Peace of His Hands* shows what riches of spirituality and unhackneyed symbolic form could be ours if we turned to the truly creative minds instead of accepting without a murmur the standardized offerings of the trade. (PLATE 24)

C. Art in the Church

The architect's work is not done when he has completed his plans for a church. It also involves close co-operation with the artists and craftsmen who are to give the church its desired accents. Everything that belongs to a church should be in keeping with the character and formal language of the edifice. Artists and craftsmen are invariably happy to work with an architect who respects their right to creative freedom within the limits of the over-all plan. They do their best when they know how their work is to fit into the whole and become a harmonious part of it. Then it will not happen that small, finely wrought statues are placed so far from the congregation as to become an indistinguishable blur, or that a stained-glass window requires artificial lighting to reveal its beauty. Incon-

gruities of this kind can be bothersome enough to make people
feel ill at ease.

The same sincerity and truth we demand of the architect
must be the guiding principle of his co-workers in the arts
and crafts. To make wood or plaster simulate costly marble,
or thin sheets of brass look like solid bronze, is to state an
untruth. There is no place in the church of Christ, we are convinced, for deception of any kind, harmless as it may seem.
In this respect our thinking differs sharply from that of the
baroque period, which conceived of the church building as a
glorious setting for the ritual of a triumphant faith. The worshiper was almost literally to be swept off his feet by the impact of forms and colors whose turbulent rhythms seemed
to leave the earth behind and ascend to higher spheres. Every
artistic and technical device was welcomed if it helped achieve
this end. The church thus became a grandiose stage where the
spiritual drama of the liturgy was enacted. Since we do not
expect stage scenery to be in reality what it represents, the
sumptous, though usually only skin-deep, decorations draped
over the church interior were not considered a deliberate
deception.

We are not called to sit in judgment over the baroque age,
but our situation compels us to affirm a different ethos. The
world in which we live is too disillusioned, and too knowing,
to take tinsel and make-believe in the house of God seriously
or even kindly. It tolerates only the truth. Any pretense of
" faked " appearance, whether of antiquity or of costly materials, we deem unworthy of the faith.

Our time also demands restraint in decorations and furnishings, and the strict avoidance of what is called " arty."
Some older churches suffer from a horror vacui: the eye cannot rest anywhere without being spoken to. In such surroundings we remember Meister Eckhart's words: " Nothing in all
creation is so like God as stillness." The eye needs areas of
silence. Modern architects therefore like to preserve large,
unbroken stretches of wall space, or to repeat without change

a simple window pattern. The resemblance of some recently built churches to those of the early Christian period is more than coincidence. The sincere plainness of these unassuming early churches is close to the heart of the contemporary designer who realizes that the purpose of a church is to serve neither as a background for pageantry, nor as a concert or lecture hall or an art gallery, but as a consecrated place of corporate worship. Liturgical churches now often stress this concept by placing the altar in the center and seating the congregation around it. It strengthens their feeling of oneness and, at the same time, makes them more active participants in the service.

It cannot be denied that some recent churches have carried simplicity almost to the point of barrenness. The reluctance to admit decorative elements, even in form of abstract designs, may stem from a reaction against overly ornate interiors of the past, or from an intellectual purism that fails to take into account the emotional needs of the people and denies them the joy that is their rightful heritage as followers of Christ. But when architect, artist, and craftsman work together in the service of God, they will make the church a worthy and helpful place of Christian worship. "This is the most beautiful cause for cultivation of the arts," Rudolf Koch once said, "when a heart overflowing with gratitude wishes to lend ornament and beauty to the lovely services of the Lord. Then the hands of the craftsmen praise the name of the Highest with the purest joy, and whosoever sees the finished work will go away blessed, be it after a thousand years." [5]

A work of Christian art — a wall painting, textured hanging, mosaic, a piece of sculpture either in the round or in relief, or a stained-glass window — can aid the worshiper, through the experience of empathy, to attune his whole being to adoration, praise, and thanksgiving. The angels surrounding the Pantocrator in Byzantine mosaics, the prophets and saints in the windows of medieval cathedrals, even the lords and ladies who kneel, a little too pompously, on many epitaphs in the baroque churches of the northern Renaissance, are silently asking all who enter to join in prayer. If we welcome the artists of our time into our churches, they will gladly add their — and our — voices to these choirs of praise, either in expressive figures or in vibrant abstract designs. Villon's windows for Metz Cathedral, the huge window wall by Emil Frei and Robert Harmon in St. Anne's Church, Normandy, Missouri, Albert Burkart's great "Creation" window in St. Joseph's, Fort Atkinson, Wisconsin, and numerous other modern masterpieces show convincingly that rhythmic forms and colors have the same power to evoke the spirit of joyful adoration as an equally abstract prelude and fugue by Johann Sebastian Bach. Sweeping, colorful designs of this kind are particularly helpful in banishing the self-consciousness that often overcomes people when they enter a church.

They arrive dressed in their Sunday clothes and are ceremoniously ushered to their seats, perhaps by a gentleman in morning coat and boutonniere. Strenuously trying to remain inconspicuous, they crowd the rear benches. They feel somehow awkward and hesitate to raise their voices in hymns and responses. The whole atmosphere is likely to keep them tightly within their shells. A church building designed to do away with undue formality helps set them free to offer themselves to God. A fine work of art clearly visible from the pews focuses thoughts apt to wander off in reverie. It prepares the individual for worship by turning his mind away from preoccupation with the self and enabling him to feel at one before God with those around him.

A large, hand-wrought altar cross set against a simple background can fulfill the function of gathering in and centering meditation both in preparation for and during the service. The usual foundry-produced metal cross, surrounded by equally standardized candle holders, is too impersonal (and generally too small) to do so. A handmade work is a bridge between persons and readily communicates the love and devotion that went into its making. The carefully considered proportions, the almost imperceptible personal touches, speak of reverence and evoke the same answer. In its simple strength such a cross reminds us of the infinite love that led Christ to Calvary. "For nails were not enough to hold God-and-man nailed and fastened to the cross, had not love held him there." (Catherine of Siena.)

As works of art express praise and adoration, they should also be designed to deepen our sense of awe before God. This contradicts popular notions of "the man upstairs" or similar attempts to encourage a kind of cozy intimacy between God and man, but the Christian church cannot bypass Jesus' word of the narrow gate and the hard way that lead to life. To give the impression that Christianity is easy is to falsify its inner meaning and weaken the power of the gospel, despite increasing numbers of names on membership rolls. Waltz rhythms and trite sentimentality in hymns and anthems destroy awe as effectively as do candy-colored plaster statues and technicolor prints of the type sold at the "religious goods" counters of dime stores, and nowadays also at roadside stands. The creative artists of our time refuse to cater to the popular and the sentimental. They know that to call forth the emotion of awe, which is the ground of faith, a work of art must make demands on the viewer. It is not to be reduced to the obvious in order to be immediately understood. Only what is shallow discloses itself to the casual glance, and talking down to the people is a worse mistake than talking over their heads. They can be trusted to accept truth with uplifted hearts, not to scorn it. Paul's admonition to be mature in thinking (I Cor. 14:20) applies to art as well, and we know that "solid food" is for the mature (Heb. 5:14). We seriously question the right or the wisdom of the church to treat believers as easily impressionable children.

Everything in art that has ever been great has been extreme, a French writer has recently observed. Yet the masters who could have renewed Christian art have with deadly monotony been rejected as extremists in their own lifetime. These obstinately repeated experiences should finally give us pause to reflect. "Today a work of artistic merit and true religious depth must of necessity at first cause a shock." [6] The responsible artist has no use for a conventional, halfhearted faith. He will not soft-pedal the impact of the gospel message, nor will he oversimplify it. There is a place for the utter simplicity of the cry for help, or the spontaneous word of gratitude. But to be able to speak a helpful word to men and women bewildered by the many-faceted personal and social problems of our time, the artist must be humbly aware of the awesome mystery of the faith. Without full recognition of the distance between God and man, art as well as worship lacks the dimension of depth and either stagnates in empty ritual or degenerates into the platitudes of "popular" religion.

The language of art contributes to the sense of awe in ways inaccessible to the reasoning mind, aside from the subject matter or meaning of a particular work. Color and form as such carry significance for us beyond the power of words to analyze. This is generally true of our sensory experiences. The fragrance of a flower, the taste of a fruit, the sensations of body balance, movement, or touch cannot be adequately articulated, much less explained. Through its rhythm and cadence a Bible passage can affect us deeply when the same thought, expressed in unrhythmical prose, might fail to do so. Rhythms of colors and forms, like those of music and poetry, are apprehended by subconscious levels of the mind. Deficiency of language makes it impossible to take into full consciousness the particular quality of a deep blue or a warm green, of straight and curved lines, or of three-dimensional shapes. The arts thus speak not only to the intellect but to the whole person, and they augment one another. From very early times poetry, rhythmic prose, music, and the visual arts have played a large role in the liturgy of the church. They can add greater depth of experience to nonliturgical services as well by providing the overtones needed if we are to live up to the command to love God with heart, soul, and mind. They help us catch a glimpse of what Paul meant when he spoke of the "fullness of God," which "was pleased to dwell" in Christ (Col. 1:19).

When art expresses praise and adoration it parallels the function of hymns, responses, and prayers. It may be compared to the confession of faith and to the proclamation and interpretation of the Word in the sermon when it deals specifically with the person of the Savior or with other Scriptural subjects. This places a great responsibility on the artist. In the past he could rely on established, traditional patterns for religious scenes. Until the end of the Middle Ages, artists worked almost exclusively for the church and had to pass through long years of apprenticeship before they were free to undertake work of their own. They were not expected to be original, and their ambition generally did not go beyond doing perhaps a little better than others what was expected of them in the framework of the current style and technique. Only the man of genius would feel emboldened to advance toward new goals and new forms.

Today the artist is in an entirely different position. A craft tradition once discarded is not easily re-established, as several unsuccessful attempts in the not-too-distant past have proved. Moreover, the artist is now called upon to create uniquely personal, original work in a style unmistakably his own. He confronts an audience that holds widely different views in regard to both art and faith and that is at the same time far more critical than at any time in the past. Yet a hesitant, fearful approach and compromise half-measures are bound to produce ephemeral work. Artist and congregation alike need to remember the stern warning: "Because you are lukewarm, and neither cold nor hot, I will spew you out of my mouth" (Rev. 3:16).

It is one of the heartening phenomena in our frequently cynical age to observe the willingness of many painters and sculptors, including some of the most famous and successful, to dedicate months or years of their best efforts to the service of the church, often at a nominal fee. What urges them on is a compelling need to bring a thank offering to the Creator for the gifts of vision and power they have received, and the conviction that the message of Christ can save a world on the brink of abyss. But in order to affect the world, the good news must be proclaimed with all its disturbing, demanding force. The days are gone when Christian art could move in the safe orbit of a lecture dealing with a past event in history. The supposedly " authentic " Arab costumes, the palm trees, and pyramids dear to the late nineteenth century have disappeared. Today's artists feel with Kierkegaard that Christ's presence on earth never becomes merely a bygone event. " So long as there is a believer, such a one must, in order to become such, have been, and as a believer must continue to be, just as contemporary with his presence on earth as were those first contemporaries. This contemporaneousness is the condition of faith, and more closely defined, it is faith." [7]

It is not necessary to put Christ and the people around him in clothing of our time to achieve this immediacy, although that has been attempted and deserves serious thought. The later Middle Ages and the untutored " folk " painters and embroiderers of the seventeenth and eighteenth centuries did not hesitate to adopt the device. However, the intended message is usually perceived most clearly when details of clothing and other accessories are kept to a minimum, suggested rather than explicitly stated. The same may be said of facial features. Several painters, among them Matisse, in the chapel he built at Vence, have even left faces entirely blank, allowing the viewer to fill them in in his imagination and trusting that sensitively drawn outlines are expressive enough. Artistic considerations should decide in each individual case, not theory. The house of modern art, like that of the Father, has many rooms. The artist has the right to choose for himself which of them he wishes to inhabit, only he must then make it his own and not try to reside in two or more rooms at the same time, the characteristic error of the eclectic.

A fine work of art also has power to give assurance and consolation. There are times in the life of every Christian when
doubts beset him, when he is near despair, or oppressed by
grief. Then even the familiar words of the service may ring
hollow, and the sermon be of little help. At such moments a
painting or sculpture, or a radiant stained-glass window, may
reveal itself to him in deep blessing. Vibrant colors and expressive forms tell of suffering heroically borne and overcome
in a language he will understand even if he cannot explain
it. Suddenly he may discover a very personal meaning, as if
the artist has spoken directly to him and his condition. Yet
at the same time, the unchangeable stillness of the painting,
its remoteness from the ticking away of the emotion-charged
minutes, may slowly help him to gain the sense of distance
that enables him to see himself and his problems in a new
perspective. The entire congregation will share this experience in times of distress.

Even in happier days a church is certain to reap a harvest
of trust and assurance if it, like the First Presbyterian Church
of Stamford, Connecticut, has the wisdom to call on creative
artists when it decides to build. The towering symbolic compositions of the crucifixion and resurrection in the unusually
folded window walls on both sides of the single-nave audi-
torium are like the strains of a mighty chorale. They bear witness to a strong, living faith unafraid to confront the age. Here,
as in a growing number of other modern churches, we are
offered convincing proof that great art can be a channel for
the communication of the Christian message.

D. Art and the Devotional Life

The corporate worship of the church expresses and affirms
its belief in the Kingdom of God both as it is already alive in
the community of the believers and as it will ultimately be
fulfilled in all creation. The individual Christian needs to par-
ticipate in corporate worship, yet his spiritual life remains at
best one-sided without personal meditation and prayer. "There

can be no Kingdom of God in the world without the Kingdom
of God in our hearts," Albert Schweitzer has said. "The start-
ing point is our determined effort to bring every thought and
action under the sway of the Kingdom of God. Nothing can
be achieved without inwardness. The Spirit of God will only
strive against the spirit of the world when it has won its victory over that spirit in our hearts." [8]

When Christian art enters the church as an aid to worship,
it affects, at the same time, the devotional life of each member
of the congregation, an additional reason why the most careful
thought should be given to the building and furnishing of a
church. But there are other ways as well for Christian art to
reach the individual. On visits to other places of worship, to
museums and galleries, on his travels, and most frequently
through reproductions in books or journals, he becomes acquainted with many works of religious painting and sculpture.
Some he is likely to reject as incompatible with his own convictions, or because he is unprepared for them. Others will
deepen his faith in unexpected and sometimes unsettling ways.
For the impact of a work of art can lead to a "shaking of the
foundations," to what is in every sense a conversion experience. It is said of Francis of Assisi that one day as he was
praying, with his eyes lifted to a painting of the crucified
Christ, he heard the Savior's voice calling him to go and re-
store his church, afflicted by the dry rot of corruption. The rich
young playboy could not dismiss the vision from his thoughts.
In a complete reversal of his former way of living he offered
himself to Christ, whose loving and beloved saintly disciple he
became. Centuries later, the Protestant Count Nikolaus von
Zinzendorf was similarly brought into the service of Christ as
the protector of the Moravian Brethren when he contemplated
a painting of the Son of Man with the crown of thorns and an
inscription reading, "This I did for you; what are you doing
for me?" [9]

Another remarkable conversion was that of Thomas Merton,
now a Trappist monk. In his autobiography, *The Seven Storey*

Mountain, he attributes the beginning of his religious life to the powerful impression of the great early Christian and Byzantine mosaics in the churches of Rome. A revealing passage deserves extensive quotation.

> After all the vapid, boring, semipornographic statuary of the Empire, what a thing it was to come upon the genius of an art full of spiritual vitality and earnestness and power — an art that was tremendously serious and alive and eloquent and urgent in all that it had to say. And it was without pretentiousness, without fakery, and had nothing theatrical about it. Its solemnity was made all the more astounding by its simplicity — and by the obscurity of the places where it lay hid, and by its subservience to higher ends, architectural, liturgical, and spiritual ends which I could not even begin to understand, but which I could not avoid guessing, since the nature of the mosaics themselves and their position and everything about them proclaimed it aloud. . . . These mosaics told me more than I had ever known of the doctrine of a God of infinite power, wisdom, and love who had yet become Man. . . . Of course I could not grasp and believe these things explicitly. But since they were implicit in every line of the pictures I contemplated with such admiration and love, surely I grasped them implicitly — I had to, in so far as the mind of the artist reached my own mind, and spoke to it his conception and his thought. And so I could not help but catch something of the ancient craftsman's love of Christ, the Redeemer and Judge of the World.[10]

Thomas Merton thereupon began reading the Bible in order to understand what these mosaics told him. Thus began his pilgrimage to God.

Rarely has a writer explained so clearly the influence of great religious art. Many other Christians owe it their spiritual awakening, but conversion extends more often over a period of time and is too gradual for the individual to attribute its onset to a particular work of art. Vincent van Gogh's words aim in this direction: "If a man loves Rembrandt profoundly, then in his heart of hearts he knows God." Perhaps no higher tribute has ever been paid by one great artist to another one. Not every person, of course, is equally affected by art. One's reaction depends on his over-all orientation and outlook on life. Of the six "types of men" Eduard Spranger distinguished (the theoretic, economic, aesthetic, social, political, and religious), the aesthetic is characterized by his deep and eager response to art. These types, however, do not occur in complete purity. The normal personality combines aspects of all of them in an infinite range of variations, though one or two tend to dominate. We do not know the proportion of primarily aesthetically oriented people in the population. It is certainly significant enough to justify greater emphasis on the visual arts by the churches, for "the religious evaluation of life always echoes in the aesthetic type." [11] If such persons fail to find the worship service or the building of their own church aesthetically satisfying, they are likely to transfer to another in search of fulfillment, or they may lose touch with the faith altogether. Great religious art can also evoke the aesthetic response in people who had allowed it to atrophy, or had suppressed it because our society has for generations relegated it to a position on the outer fringes of its concerns.

A carefully chosen work of Christian art can mean a great deal for a family. Unobtrusively, in many imperceptible ways it will affect each of its members, encourage devotion and commitment, and influence their moral attitude. The habit of giving thanks to God at mealtime is more easily established or continued when such a work graces the home. It invites quietness and reflection, and helps us to trust. As a constant reminder of the things of God it will in part fill the void that now yawns in the religious life of far too many Christians between one Sunday morning service and the next. And who can foresee if a visible token of the faith may not, in a critical hour when the very life of the family hangs in the balance, become a means of grace and a blessing?

Those who have lived with a fine work of Christian art know how much it benefits their spiritual life. It can have especially

great value for ministers and other professional religious
workers. The greatest danger of their constant occupation
with matters of faith is staleness, a fading of the inspiration.
Laymen cannot easily appreciate what it means to a clergy-
man, for instance, to prepare a new sermon week after week,
not to mention the unending administrative chores. Such men
and women will derive a real blessing from being able to rest
their eyes for a while on a fine painting or print, and to re-
fresh the spirit by quiet contemplation. Conflicts and difficulties seem less dark when one has meditated on the deeper
truth of a worshipful design. Whether they prefer the timeless
fervor of a Byzantine icon, Fra Angelico's sweet grace, Rembrandt's vision of Christ's compassionate love, or a dynamic
contemporary work, they whose task and high privilege is the
proclamation of the gospel will feel as grateful to the artist
as the thirsty wanderer is for a drink of clear water. A minister, of all people, should choose wisely what is to become part
of his personal environment. Called to be Christ's interpreter
to souls in need of a saving faith, he cannot be too insistent in
his demand for truth in a work of art lest he, unwittingly, become prey to the fallacy of poetizing Christ.

E. The Didactic Function of Christian Art

Teaching (*didachē*) and proclamation (*kērygma*) are in-
separable in the New Testament. In the same way, every work
of art that proclaims a Christian truth has a didactic value.
Christian leaders from earliest times have accepted this teaching function of art even when they opposed its use as an aid
in the worship of the church. Scenes from the Scriptures displayed on walls and in windows were intended as a Bible for
the illiterate. They often reveal a wide, detailed knowledge of
the Old and New Testaments and the Apocrypha and served
for the instruction of the catechumens and the young. The
Reformation recognized the value of the visual approach by
producing copiously illustrated Bibles. Translations into almost every language were adorned with woodcuts or engrav-

ings meant to inspire as well as to teach. (Among the books thus illustrated is the first book for children to be published in America, the *History of the Holy Jesus*.)

A curious book printed in 1899 under the title *Picture Puzzles, or How to Read the Bible by Symbols* shows to what length the attempt to teach through images could be carried. Its professed aim was to "stimulate a greater interest in the Holy Bible" among boys and girls, but whether it achieved this aim is open to doubt. Each page has several engravings, illustrations rather than symbols as the title implies, with a few connecting words. When correctly interpreted, they give short Scriptural passages, some as familiar as the Twenty-third Psalm, others apparently culled at random from little known books of the Bible. One page, for instance, pictures part of Zech. 12:6; another, Judg. 5:25 and half of verse 26: "He asked water, and she gave him milk; she brought forth butter in a lordly dish. She put her hand to the nail, and her right hand to the workman's hammer." The words "water," "milk," "dish," "hand," and "workman" have to be guessed from the illustrations. The point of the quotation, when Jael strikes the blow to crush Sisera's head, is missing. Obviously, it was not considered the right thing for young people. Why any child should have to decipher and possibly memorize disjointed, meaningless fragments remains a mystery. The book is an intriguing oddity. It proves that a useful idea becomes absurd when applied to teach the letter instead of the spirit of the Word.

Old-fashioned methods of Christian education, marked by inadequate consideration for the psychological problem of the learner and his motivation and by the crushing burden of literal-mindedness, have no doubt contributed to the amazing religious illiteracy of the average modern Christian, adult or young alike. The same people who are willing to spend many hours learning about the ideas and rituals of their fraternal organizations rarely ever touch a book about the Christian faith (unless they are pressed into service as Sunday church school teachers), and know little about its basic facts, including the life and teachings of the Savior. We can only hope that the new and far more readable Bible translations, and a much greater recognition of the need for adult education in the churches, may in time correct this glaring deficiency.

But even young people fresh out of years of Sunday church school, in the great majority, are unfamiliar with the major events related in the Scriptures, as many a college teacher has discovered. Something is decidedly wrong in our Christian education when so many men, women, and young people have only the haziest acquaintance with the Bible, not to mention the history of the church. There is small wonder that so many Christians cling without much conviction to vague, platitudinous concepts of the Savior and his message. Religious leaders and educators have naturally been greatly concerned. Constant efforts are being made to establish new goals and teaching methods and to improve the available curricular materials.[12]

A major problem in religious education is how to combine the presentation and learning of the story as a historical fact with the need to involve the learner in its spiritual, moral, and ethical implications to the point of personal commitment. As Iris V. Cully has stated, " Since the _kērygma_ is not a set of abstract propositions but is the record of God's saving activity in history, it must be spoken in such a way that the event is remembered and made _contemporary_." [13]

Animated filmstrips, movies, or comic-strip type illustrations often fall short of the goal by distracting the learner's attention from the center of the story. They either swerve too quickly into applications supposedly closer to the child's range of experience, or unfold the story in a series of images that pass by far too rapidly to permit concentrated study and exploration. The child is perhaps entertained, but not instructed. Unless such visual aids are of the highest quality (which invariably means, artistic), he will remember them no better than the numerous television programs he watches in the course of the week. Most adults, too, retain little of a film or television show, just as they quickly forget the cartoons and news photos in the daily papers.

The effect of a great work of art is entirely different, whether it is shown in the original or as a print of sufficient size, a color slide or in a filmstrip. The main point is that it holds still, a true blessing in itself. It invites concentration, careful observation, and discussion. Some members of the group will delight in pointing out details others may have overlooked.

The study of a work of art, in contrast to serial or moving pictures, permits a correction of hasty, first impressions. The viewers come to identify themselves, through the process of empathy, with the various personalities whose facial expressions or gestures reveal their emotions as the artist has observed and felt them himself. There is no "play acting" in a great work of Christian art. To choose anything else for study not only would waste precious time but can establish the false conceptions of the faith that Christian education is trying to combat. An unhurried exploration of a true masterpiece, not carried, of course, to the point of boredom or exhaustion, involves each participant in a highly personal encounter with truth.

It also ensures a vivid memory of the work of art and its message. The chief reason why it is so much better remembered than photographs or moving pictures is its quality of form. The photographic lens records every aspect of reality with the same clarity and sharpness, whereas the artist selects and combines the essential elements to create his design. We need not be consciously aware of the formal structure of the work to be strongly affected by it, and the church school is not the place for a detailed analysis. When the children's admiration is aroused and they wonder how the artist achieved his aim, they will quite naturally begin to look for the main features of the composition. By covering any part of it, they will discover how important it is for the whole. In Rembrandt's etching *Christ Preaching*, for instance, we may see only a casual grouping of figures until we realize that not one is superfluous. Each fills its place in the over-all design to lead the eye around Christ, who yet remains the center, visually as well as spiritually.

The investigations of the Gestalt school of psychology (best translated "configuration") have produced ample evidence for the apparently innate tendency of the human mind to organize sensory stimuli in entities, or configurations, in order to make them meaningful. The formal organization, or structure, of a work of art enables us to see it as a Gestalt, sharply differentiated from its unstructured background. It is therefore much more easily remembered. From this viewpoint, too, art becomes an invaluable aid for Christian education. Incidents or stories that otherwise might not fully congeal into mental images are consolidated and can become part of ourselves. The Biblical authors, like all great poets, must have had an intuitive knowledge of this principle when they phrased their stories in an intensely graphic style replete with superb imagery. The church recognized almost from its beginnings that the visual arts have the same power of condensing thought and making it poignant. For the many religiously illiterate Christians of our time they could once again become a bridge to the Bible.

We need not fear that great art is too difficult for children or young people. Many parts of the Scriptures, especially of the Gospels, are by no means easy to interpret; yet we must acquaint our children with them in the hope of laying the groundwork for future enlightenment and spiritual growth. Children are less inhibited in their imagination and less fixed in their taste than are adults. They approach masterpieces of the most varied periods and styles with keen interest. What looks baffling to adults does not seem strange to them. But they are also sharp critics of the superficial and the insincere. Polite conventions mean little to them; what they want is the truth. They will receive lasting impressions and gain insights that no textbook can communicate, even if they cannot penetrate to the deepest levels of meaning. Truly great art is inexhaustible; once our eyes and hearts have been opened to it, we shall return to it, later, and, with minds matured by experience, discover the fuller measure of its message.

Chapter IV

Scope and Limits
of Christian Art

A work of art that is not good and true in art is not good or true in any other respect and is useless for any purpose whatsoever — even for edification.
— Dorothy Sayers.

A. The Christian Artist

If we accept Paul Tillich's definition of faith as ultimate concern, we can say that all great art is religious at its core. Unless the artist deals with ultimate concerns in his creative efforts, he is a mere entertainer, a juggler of forms and colors. When the term " religious " is taken in this widest sense, there is no essential difference between a painting representing the Madonna, a landscape, or a still life of flowers, provided the painter was capable of emulating John Constable, of whom it has been said that he worked so lovingly and tenaciously as " to make the contrasted sparkle and gloom of nature in a small part of one county stand as a symbol for the sparkle and gloom of the world and of eternity." [1]

The Christian who has kept himself free of bigotry can fully appreciate the spiritual, indeed the " religious " values of all great art. What has been created out of love will evoke in the observer a perception of the life-affirming values of beauty, order, and truth. These values testify to the God-ordained relationship between man and the created world. To recognize them is to refute the helpless despair expressed in Albert

Camus' phrase concerning the "benign indifference of the universe."

At the same time, the Christian can object that "religious" is too unspecific a term for the art of the church. It includes the most widely differing faiths, from polytheism to humanism. Protestants, however, hesitate to use the term "sacred" art. They feel that "sacred" should be used only in reference to the realities chosen by God to reveal himself to man: the Word and the sacraments. "A building, a communion table, baptismal fonts, either contribute by their beauty to the praise which the church offers to its Lord, or oppose themselves to it by their ugliness, but they are not 'sacred objects.'" [2] This is equally true of paintings, statuary, or stained-glass windows. We may call the stories recorded in them "sacred" in so far as they are based on Scripture, but the term does not apply to the works of art as such. When directly serving the worship of the church or enhancing its ritual and dogma, we may refer to them as "liturgical" art — a term that, in turn, makes them often objectionable to nonliturgical churches.

Perhaps we could fall back on the term "Christian" art. It is broader than "sacred" or "liturgical," narrower than "religious." However, it should be used with care, and without the self-righteous claims often associated with the use of the adjective "Christian" in politics and economics. It is best understood in the sense in which we speak of Christian vocations in agriculture, medicine, the law, education, social work, homemaking, industry, and commerce. No person has the right to claim this term unless he is ready to accept responsibilities over and above the customary demands and standards of his profession or occupation, and intends to dedicate his or her best efforts not to self-aggrandizement but to the service of God and neighbor. We are justified in speaking of a Christian vocation only when we endeavor to apply the teachings of the Savior to the problems of our daily work and the decisions we are called to make, when the service principle inspires our every thought and act.

Such service in obedience to the faith is neither servitude nor an "escape from freedom." On the contrary, as D. M. Baillie has lucidly explained, man finds highest fulfillment in it, thanks to the paradox of grace: "Never is human action more truly and fully personal, never does the agent feel more perfectly free, than in those moments of which he can say as a Christian that whatever good was in them was not his but God's." [3] We can call a work of art Christian when it is illumined by the spirit of the Christian *kērygma*. Its origin or point of reference must be the Gospels, for Christianity as a revealed faith affirms: "In the beginning was the Word, and the Word was with God, and the Word was God" (John 1:1). Herein lies the distinction between religious art in general and Christian art. For whatever purpose a work is intended — as an aid to worship, for private devotion, for instruction, or as a song of praise, a token of love, it is Christian only when it relates itself to the spirit of the New Testament. This may raise difficult problems considering the varying, sometimes conflicting interpretations of the Gospels from apostolic times on. The thinking of past ages does not always correspond to our views. Still, the churches of Christ are in agreement on certain basic tenets. They worship God as Creator of the universe and of man. They believe that he is infinite wisdom, power, justice, and love, that he has revealed himself to man first through patriarchs and prophets, later and most fully in the person of Jesus Christ, and still reveals himself through the Holy Spirit to those who turn to him in faith. The churches recognize man's sinfulness and his need for the redemption that God freely offers him. They look with confidence to the coming of his Kingdom. All accept the truth of Jesus' words: "You shall love the Lord your God with all your heart, and with all your soul, and with all your mind. This is the great and first commandment. And a second is like it, You shall love your neighbor as yourself. On these two commandments depend all the law and the prophets" (Matt. 22:37-40).

Only on these foundations, with faith, hope, and love as the motivating energies, can Christian life and art be built. Any tendency to deify man himself, any of his groups or social concepts, or anything material, is non-Christian. So is the glorification of hate, lust, or despair. While the Christian artist is fully aware of man's fallen state and the tragic conflicts tormenting him, he also knows of the light behind the darkness. "No purely tragic work can be in the order of redemption, for it is only tragedy redeemed that can be fully loyal to the redeeming Lord." [4] To see sensitive artists so obsessed by the inhumanity of our civilization as to create the nightmarish paintings and sculptures recently shown in an exhibition entitled "New Images of Man" is an indictment of the failure of the churches to proclaim to our time Christ's saving message of love. When theologians defend nuclear armaments or the injustice of racial segregation (*apartheid*), this message is weakened and corroded. We need then not be surprised at the statement of one artist: "The inclusion of the phrase 'Please Leave Me Alone' on the back of St. Sebastian the Second, . . . is an arrow aimed at compassion," [5] at the prevalence of fetishes and totemistic forms, or the preoccupation with decay and corruption of all physical matter. "At the limits of reason," one perceptive critic has written, "one comes face to face with the meaningless; and the artist today shows us the absurd, the inexplicable, the meaningless in our daily life." [6]

Here, indeed, is the parting of the ways. At the limits of reason the believing Christian comes face to face not with meaninglessness but with the all-embracing love of God. He is ready to answer, with George Fox: "When all my hopes in all men were gone, so that I had nothing outwardly to help me, nor could I tell what to do; then, oh then, I heard a voice which said, 'There is one, even Christ Jesus, that can speak to thy condition': and when I heard it, my heart did leap for joy." There is no question that some of the *avant-garde* artists represented in the exhibition, and others working in a similar vein, are sincerely convinced of the need for violent protest to bring us face to face with our real situation and enable us to build anew. In others we sense a true despair that the experience of love could one day transmute into the assurance of the psalmist:

> If I say, " Let only darkness cover me,
>   and the light about me be night,"
> even the darkness is not dark to thee.
>   (Ps. 139: 11-12.)

In the case of other artists (and writers) of today, however, we wonder if their despair is not a subtle form of *hubris,* related to the all-or-nothing attitude of the neurotic. There is self-pity in it, the agony of the bitterly disappointed belief in man's capacity to achieve perfection by his own power. Nor is it a unique phenomenon of our time. We find it foreshadowed in parts of Michelangelo's *Last Judgment,* in Goya, Munch, and Ensor. The Christian understanding of man sees his limitations far more realistically and recognizes pride as the cardinal sin from which all others spring. " Despair," wrote Thomas Merton, " is the ultimate development of a pride so great and so stiff-necked that it selects the absolute misery of damnation rather than accept happiness from the hands of God and thereby acknowledge that he is above us and that we are not capable of fulfilling our destiny by ourselves." [7] At the same time, the Christian knows that no man can commit a sin so great as to exhaust the infinite love of God.

Christian art stands in the service of the faith but can gratefully accept the offerings of creative minds outside the organized churches. The convinced atheist, of course, will remain aloof. But some artists respond to the person and the teachings of the Savior even though they have been brought up in a different tradition or have become alienated from the church through personal disappointments. To them, Christ's word applies: "Whoever does the will of my Father in heaven is my brother, and sister, and mother " (Matt. 12:50). He did not turn away the Roman centurion who came to him with sincere respect. Thoughtful Christians have applauded the decision of Anglican and Roman Catholic leaders to enlist the freely offered co-operation of Jewish artists such as Chagall and Sir John Epstein, or of agnostics like the painters Léger and Matisse and the sculptor Lambert-Rucki.

Pie Raymond Régamey, a French Dominican in the front rank of Roman Catholic theologians concerned about the Christian art of our time, emphatically defends this view. "When men of good will attest by their works the admirable powers they have to serve the church, it is outrageous . . . to see Christians with peremptory levity, in the name of their faith, object to the flowers and fruits this very faith brings forth in ground deemed capable only of bearing thorns." [8] We may add that working for a church many rekindle an artist's personal faith or lead him to a conversion experience.

An added reason why Christians can rejoice when men outside the church dedicate their best efforts to enhance its message is the undeniable fact that nominal Christians among the artists of the past have been guilty of glib and unconvincing lip service. It would be entirely unrealistic to assume a truly living faith as the force behind every one of the thousands of paintings and sculptures almost mass-produced from the later Middle Ages on. Not a few are mere routine work ground out by large workshops in monotonous repetition of the same arrangements, and can boast of little more than decorative value. Some of the most famous masters were at best "fringe" Christians and painted religious subjects simply in order to earn their livelihood. We hear of Perugino that he had "little religion and did not believe in immortality. He trusted only in fortune and would do anything for money." [9] That did not prevent him from producing religious scenes of cloying sentimentality, once uncritically admired. Benozzo Gozzoli has been called a skeptic; Fra Filippo Lippi is known for his licentious living; and so forth. Churches and museums preserve a great deal of uninspired work of poor quality, though curators increasingly try to relegate it to their storerooms so as to give uncrowded space to their really valuable possessions. In sharp contrast, a responsible artist of our time who is not a church member professes sincere respect for and sympathy with the truth of the Christian proclamation when he chooses a Christian subject.

We can also profit from the contributions of artists who use Christian themes to express a strong social concern. Contemporary painters have repeatedly turned to the crucifixion to register their abhorrence of man's inhumanity to man. The figure they show broken on the cross may be Everyman rather than Christ, but Christians cannot disregard a passionate spiritual anger when it lashes out against evil with the vehemence of the prophets of old. A striking example is a mural by the Mexican painter José Clemente Orozco at Dartmouth College. Timid souls and "Sunday" Christians may shrink from the fierce vision and call it blasphemy, but others will recognize its bitter truth. A towering Christ stands astride a large cross that he has felled with his ax. Rightful wrath blazes from his eyes against those who, calling themselves his followers, have betrayed him and his message by forging and using the murderous weapons piled up in a heap behind him — guns, mortars, tanks. Tom Loftin Johnson's *American Pieta* shows the aftermath of a lynching, with the Negro family mourning the victim. The painter used the medieval theme of Christ's mother holding her dead son in her arms to bring home to us the full implications of the brutal act. Did not Jesus say in his great parable of the judgment, "As you did it to one of the least of these my brethren, you did it to me" (Matt. 25:40)? (PLATE 25)

The serious Christian cannot see works of this kind without being stirred to repentance. By awakening in us a deeper awareness of our involvement in mankind, of our share in the burden of guilt for our neighbor's suffering, they relate themselves to the Christian message. That is why Paul Tillich could call Picasso's great *Guernica* mural a "truly Protestant" painting. "There you see the world in pieces, and that's the one side which Protestantism always . . . must emphasize. It's not the whole of Protestantism, but . . . what is nearest to our present mind is just this side." [10]

Socially conscious art is not always Christian art. But when it stems from sincere compassion, it can be an invaluable corrective for a self-centered faith that fails to judge society by the standards of Christ and proceeds as if injustice, war, poverty, and hunger were part of the eternal plan of creation. It reminds us that God is Lord of all life, that of the community as well as that of the individual. If the grace of God can bring redemption to the most wretched sinner, we have no right to doubt that it can do as much for the community of men. Walter Rauschenbusch declared, "Whoever sets any bounds for the reconstructive power of the religious life over the social relations and institutions of man, to that extent denies the faith of the Master." [11]

The socially conscious artist of the twenties and thirties was not a lonely prophet calling in the wilderness. His work contributed to the change of climate that enabled the nation to move toward greater social justice. But the younger generation shows little of the zeal of their elders. Some are weltering in existential despair; others explore the possibilities of an art free of the subject, an art purely of form, color, and texture.

Abstract or abstract-expressionist art, the dominant style at the present, can evoke a variety of moods, from joy and exaltation to conflict, fear, and dejection. It has been successfully introduced into modern church buildings, in particular for the design of stained-glass windows. We cannot yet tell, however, whether it can become a vehicle for the proclamation of the Christian message and produce valid statements. If art is Christian, in so far as it serves the Word of God, it may require clearly defined content rather than a generalized mood, even one of adoration and thanksgiving. We know from music, often compared to abstract art because of a similar lack of subject matter, how unspecific moods can be. We tend to ascribe a religious meaning to what we often hear in a church setting, regardless of the composer's actual intent. Well-known ex-

amples are Handel's "Largo" and Bach's "Sheep Can Safely
Graze." The former was written for the opera *Xerxes;* the latter, for a birthday cantata in form of a classical allegory where
it was sung by a goddess of flocks. Neither was composed with
any thought of Christian content. Yet some rhythms and harmonies, both auditory and visual, have the power to touch the
soul and prepare it, as it were, for the reception of a religious
message. Abstract art may one day play a role in the church
similar to organ music. Besides, it should seriously recommend
itself to those who interpret the Second Commandment as
strictly excluding any figurative or representational art. Future developments will tell if abstract forms can reach the
heart of the *kērygma* and call forth the response of personal
decision and commitment. Perhaps a synthesis of the objective
and nonobjective approach will ultimately be achieved.

In the age-old debate between form and content, Christian
art must assign greater weight to content. Forms vary, and
each period of history finds its preferred systems, "but the
word of our God will stand forever" (Isa. 40:8). To grant
form equal significance with content would raise art to equal-
ity with faith, a claim Christians cannot support. There is thus
no room in Christian art for the concept of "art for art's sake."
No work of Christian art is adequately judged, or discussed,
solely in terms of its formal organization, that is, from the artistic point of view, vital as it is. To the church, the work of
art must always be a means, not an end in itself.

With the primacy of Christian content goes the imperative
need to communicate it, the main justification for Christian
art. The artist is right in demanding concentrated thought on
the part of the viewer, but does well to remember Paul's distinction between "speaking in tongues" and "prophesying."
Without rejecting the former outright, the apostle left no
doubt that he valued prophetic utterance more highly. As musical instruments are useless if they do not produce clear, distinct tones, so speech that is unintelligible is spoken into
empty air. "If I pray in a tongue, my spirit prays but my mind

is unfruitful. What am I to do? I will pray with the spirit and I will pray with the mind also; I will sing with the spirit and I will sing with the mind also." (I Cor. 14:14-15.)

There is no better advice for the Christian artist too. Where others are free to play with forms and ideas and to address themselves, if they so wish, to a small coterie of the like-minded, the Christian artist is asked to discipline himself to the constant search for communication. To fulfill his calling, he must speak in a language of forms that permits persons of good will and sensitivity to catch at least a glimpse of the truth he wants to share with them. He will be alert to new insights and new forms in which to state them, because he cannot speak to the needs of the present age if his mind is attuned only to the past. But neither he nor the church is under any obligation to be leader of the artistic fashion parade or to fall in line with every fad. If the artist, following Paul's exhortation, works with spirit and mind, he will help others to deeper understanding and a more vital faith, but he can scarcely hope to serve the Word if he speaks in an unknown "tongue." Moreover, as the Christian faith is insep-arable from the person of Jesus Christ, the reality of the incar-nation can become true experience only by means of reference to the human body. T. S. Eliot's warning, "You must not deny the body," is directed to the Christian artist also.

Yet precisely when art approaches the mystery of the in-carnation, it faces its most serious limitations. While Paul could take courage from walking "by faith, not by sight" (II Cor. 5:7), the artist's entire work depends on the sense of sight, and the deepest truths of the faith elude the reach of the senses. The spiritual concepts of redemption, salvation, grace, rebirth, eternal life, sin, guilt, and forgiveness, even hope, love, and faith itself, difficult enough to define in words, will disclose themselves to the believer in his own poignant experience. Art can approach them only indirectly by showing how they affect human beings, or suggest them by means of the symbol.

B. Reality and Symbol

Nothing illustrates the dilemma of Christian art so clearly as its attempts to create an image of God. Christian art of the first thousand years wisely refrained from it; later it represented the Creator in the image of the Second Person of the Trinity, and finally as the white-bearded patriarch. We feel today that in so doing, Christian art underestimated the effect of any image in limiting a spiritual concept to a circumscribed visual form. To represent is to particularize; yet God is boundless, in the fullest sense, illimitable. The painter can show "a" man, not Man as genus; "a" god, not God. Even Michelangelo's titanic genius could not go beyond human measure, and had to fail. The all-too-frequent representations of God the Father as the Ancient of Days are to us examples of a misguided piety. Since few Christians today are familiar with the symbolism of The Book of Daniel from which the image was originally derived (Dan. 7:9, 13, 22), a picture of a benevolent elderly man with long, white beard and flowing hair unfortunately suggests to them merely a Santa Claus.

The Bible word, "Then God said: 'Let us make man in our image'" (Gen. 1:26) has long since been understood as referring to man's spiritual, not his physical, being. It does not entitle us to reverse the process and create God in man's image. The need to visualize God is a characteristic sign of spiritual immaturity, prevalent among primitive people and children. This explains why the Hebrews had to be sternly warned against giving way to it. To the mature in faith, the Second Commandment simply states the fact that the human mind cannot conceive an image of God that could in any way be adequate. The commandment can still prove a helpful deterrent when we are tempted to yield to the desire to help persons to "see" God.

Perhaps out of the efforts of contemporary abstract artists new, inspiring symbols of God may grow in the end. The older symbols, the Tetragrammaton (the Hebrew signs for the name of God), the eye, or the triangle, are scarcely meaningful to the people of our day. We have moved far from the desire for realistic symbols and are beginning to respond to abstract designs suggesting power, movement, light, the creative energies of the cosmos that embrace and sustain every living creature. Here lies a real challenge for artists and churches. The *mysterium tremendum* of the faith, which has eluded all attempts to describe it in terms of representation, may in our time again become a living experience through the concentrated power of symbolic expression.

Literally speaking, a symbol is a mark or token. It stands for something other than itself and participates, as Paul Tillich explains, in its power and meaning by "opening levels of reality which otherwise are hidden and cannot be grasped in any other way."[12] We live in a "symbolic universe" to which language, myth, and religion belong, though familiarity has dulled our consciousness of it. The language of faith takes words descriptive of sensory experience and fills them with symbolic meaning. When the Bible speaks of God's face, arms, hands, or eyes, or uses terms like way, gate, vine, lamb for the Savior, it obviously does not want them understood in their literal sense. This is likewise true of words like high, above, ascend, descend, heaven, the throne, seated at the right hand, and other expressions. A number of the leading philosophers, psychologists, and theologians of recent years have demonstrated the surpassing significance of symbolism for man's mental and spiritual life. Tom F. Driver states frankly, "The Christian faith is not communicated except in terms of symbol."[13]

The incarnation changed man's relationship to the world around him. When God became man in Jesus Christ, everything in creation assumed a new and personal meaning, more fully so than the human mind can understand, for "now we see in a mirror dimly" and know only in part. To the early Christians, all things pointed to God, were his signposts, so to speak, and this is what constitutes their symbolic significance. From this world view grew the rich visual symbolism of the church, until it formed, in the later Middle Ages, a "cathedral of ideas," a ceaseless "transfusion of the feeling for God's majesty and eternity into everything perceptible and thinkable." Nothing was too humble to symbolize and glorify the sublime. "Symbolism opened up all the wealth of religious conceptions to art, to be expressed in forms full of color and melody, and yet vague and implicit, so that by these the profoundest intuitions might soar toward the ineffable." [14]

This all-pervading symbolism demanded very considerable theological learning, far more than the laity can ever have possessed. Even today, despite painstaking research, some of medieval symbolism in art still escapes interpretation. Near the close of the Middle Ages, objects or incidents were overburdened with meaning until they might stand for unrelated, not infrequently conflicting, ideas. Symbolism fell into disrepute when the Reformers castigated its excesses, blaming it for the spread of false doctrine and corrupt practices. It returned for a period of time in the intellectual game of the emblems and survives in the ritual of fraternal organizations, insignia of the Armed Forces, trade-marks of commerce and industry, and certain stereotyped figures and designs dear to the political cartoonist. One reason for the decline was the overly realistic representation of the symbols of faith. To suggest a higher meaning, something has to be left to the subconscious response. The closer the artist approaches the visual reality of an object, the more difficult it becomes to see it as anything else; finally, the symbolic significance disappears entirely.

These developments have caused an erosion of the sense of symbolism. Many of the old Christian symbols are no longer understood. When a group of church women some years ago met in a coastal town in Massachusetts and received name tags in the shape of the fish (or *ichthus*), they mistook them for the symbol of Massachusetts, "home of the cod." An Army officer, irritated by criticism directed at the choice of patron saints by some units of the Armed Forces, wrote that St. Barbara was " just a symbol " and " might have been a Greek god or a pagan." Apparently, neither the idea of sainthood nor the person of St. Barbara meant anything to him. The term " symbol " has become the equivalent for insigne or decorative identification tag.

Even the cross, last remaining symbol of the Christian faith to be universally understood, appears to have lost some of its full value. In the eyes of many people it stands simply for the Christian church as an organization and its activities, with little more emotional effect than the Red Cross sign, the Blue Cross sign of hospital insurance, or the red feather of the community chest campaign. " Crusades " are being mounted for — or against — practically everything under the sun. The atomization of the Protestant churches, and their narrow parochialism, have no doubt contributed to this sad state of affairs. All the valiant efforts of died-in-the-wool denominational partisans to the contrary, the vast majority of Christians today cannot become aroused about Congregationalism, Methodism, or the many others, as witnessed by their perfect willingness to transfer when changing their place of residence and finding no church of their own denomination nearby.

Yet with all his skepticism, modern man wants to believe. Many of the spiritually homeless reach out for the oversimplified affirmations of fringe sects, the more so as some of the older churches seem to have withdrawn into isolation, relying on the " loyal remnant " for their continued existence and remaining aloof from the outside world and its problems. But other churches are making a real effort to proclaim the gospel in a new, dynamic language and through new symbolic forms, recognizing that many of the old ones are worn out and beyond revival. Jesus rightly warned against putting new wine into old wineskins, and does the psalmist not call on us to " sing to the Lord a new song "?

Our time urgently demands a rediscovery of the meaning of

the holy and its potent visualization. Halos mean little to us and may even arouse suspicion. Christian artists know of the need for a new approach, for exploration and the bold search for adequate, meaningful symbols. But their creative ventures could be smothered by the sheer weight of our heritage. Every major work of Christian art that has come down to us from the past reflects a stage in the history of the faith and is therefore worthy of careful study and preservation in an appropriate setting. But the living church has the right, in fact, the duty, to discriminate between what has a vital message for our time and what is dead, and it is under no obligation whatever to treat older Christian art with the objectivity of the art historian or the museum curator. Churches are neither art museums nor graduate seminars in the history of theology.

C. The Past Outgrown

Anyone studying Christian art of the past will be surprised to discover how much of it can no longer be reconciled with the spirit of the gospel of Christ as our time understands it. Some highly valued masterpieces of painting and sculpture, undoubtedly important in the history of Western art, have become as embarrassing to Christians of the twentieth century as some of the strange concepts expounded in older theological literature. It is difficult to believe how far dedicated Christians in their zeal could stray from the clear intent of Christ's message of love. Obviously, our discrimination relates to the spiritual rather than to the aesthetic qualities of the works in question, not a few of which figure among the starred attractions in museums and churches, mainly of Europe. Their prominent display, and the fame of their makers, all too often impress Christian laymen to the extent that they silence their rightful misgivings, though they would rise in protest were a preacher to voice similar doctrines or ideas in his sermon.

A thorough, critical survey from the viewpoint of contemporary Christian thought remains to be written. Entire groups of subjects can already be seen as no longer spiritually valid or even, in some cases, defensible. We may enumerate them in six categories:

1. Purely legendary and anecdotal incidents without historical foundation, especially when of a morbid, unwholesome character or when likely to stir up antagonism against other Christian or non-Christian groups. This should not include poetic fables expressing a naïve love for sacred personages as long as they are clearly treated as legends.

2. Religious imagery unsupported by Scripture or in direct conflict with it. Representations of the Holy Trinity as a three-faced head, as two men with a dove between them, or as three men of the same physical appearance — a very frequent subject in the Middle Ages — tend to destroy the ineffable mystery of the Three-in-One. Former generations may have understood them as symbols of the love uniting the three "persons" of the Godhead, but our time sees merely three separate entities.

To show God appearing to Moses in the burning bush, or Moses looking at God, violates the spirit of the account in Ex. 3:1-6, where Moses hides his face, "for he was afraid to look at God." Neither Christ's taking leave of his mother at the outset of the Passion nor his appearance to her after the resurrection has Scriptural authority. The same must be said of Mary's life prior to the annunciation and of her death, assumption, and coronation. (The Roman Catholic Church has based the dogmas of the immaculate conception and the assumption of Mary on long tradition originating in apocryphal writings.)

3. Symbols, symbolic scenes, and allegories derived from literal interpretation of a passage in the Bible or long-forgotten, prescientific ideas about natural phenomena. The majority of these date from the Middle Ages, and many come from the *Physiologus*, the most popular compendium of medieval nature lore. To these belong such symbols of Christ as the phoenix, lion, eagle, or gryphon. The lamb too has become a symbol of doubtful value, especially when shown standing on

an altar, with blood running from its side into a chalice. This scene, like other visualizations of the imagery in The Revelation to John, looks too strange to the average person today to communicate religious insights, even when presented as appealingly as on the great Ghent altar of the Brothers van Eyck. Another example is Christ in the winepress treading the grapes (symbolic of the Eucharist), often with blood spurting from his wounds. It was taken from Isa. 63:3: " I have trodden the wine press alone . . . ," but like similar applications of isolated passages in the Old Testament, it is now understood only by the erudite. The same is true of numerous virginity symbols like the sealed fountain, the closed door, the clean towel, and the elaborate unicorn allegories.

The fantastic beasts and birds described in the *Physiologus* or the often-copied bestiaries, and freely used in medieval art as symbols of virtues and vices or of sacred personalities, are now, of course, entirely meaningless.

4. Detailed representations of the physical sufferings of the condemned sinners in hell, and of devils as fiendish monsters. Christians know the full reality of evil but have come to understand " hell " as the state of estrangement from God, as spiritual agony. They will not believe that the loving Father of mankind would decree or tolerate the sadistic tortures medieval and Renaissance artists depicted with great relish. Jesus' references to the " everlasting fire " can readily be interpreted in a figurative sense. Besides, we seriously question whether repulsive images of this kind can scare people into repentance, and doubt its value if they could. Scenes of this nature have done the faith considerable harm. Not abject fear, but love for the Savior and a sincere desire to follow in his ways are valid motivations for Christian living and can lead to true penitence and regeneration. The whole concept of the devil as a hideous specter has become farcical.

To show the blessed ones in heaven is equally futile and unacceptable unless the artist is inspired by the most tender, poetic imagination. The lovely vision of the heavenly Jerusalem, where the ransomed will walk in their golden slippers on streets paved with gold and make joyful music to the Lord, has given consolation to numberless souls thirsting for justice and peace. It has enriched the music and literature of many nations, and works of art created in this spirit will be cherished as expressions of childlike love and trust. But when painters or sculptors tried to visualize the life in the beyond in realistic terms, they failed to heed Paul's explicit warnings against the urge to know the unknowable: "I tell you this, brethren: flesh and blood cannot inherit the kingdom of God, nor does the perishable inherit the imperishable" (I Cor. 15:50).

5. Incidents from the Old Testament books reflecting a primitive stage of man's moral development at variance with the teachings of Christ. The main reason why the stories of Lot and his daughters, Bathsheba in her bath, Jael killing Sisera, Judah and Tamar, or Judith with the head of Holofernes were so often represented in earlier art is their erotic or "sensational" appeal. Without lengthy explanations they cannot convey any religious truth to Christians of the present day.

6. Scenes of martyrdoms emphasizing their most gruesome aspects. Our time is not more squeamish, nor does it lack respect for Christian martyrs (in so far as it remembers them), but is acutely conscious of how much innocent blood has been shed by Christians even in the name of their faith. Besides, the countless victims of man's inhumanity to man in our own generation are too powerful an indictment of our supposedly Christian civilization for us to gain spiritually from the sight of horrors inflicted on the martyrs. Such scenes present a dangerous temptation to forget our own involvement in guilt and responsibility. We also doubt that graphically depicted sufferings of the saints will encourage other Christians to emulate their steadfastness. Here again we can follow the wise example of the earliest Christian art which did not indulge in scenes of this nature. What our time asks to be shown most

of all is how the saints lived their faith rather than the mode of their dying for it.

Aside from these six groups of subjects, individual churches will naturally consider as unacceptable works of art glorifying doctrines contrary to their beliefs. Examples are the images of the "sacred heart" and of the miracles performed by Mary or the saints. Some Protestant denominations question the Scriptural basis for the Anastasis, or Christ's descent into Sheol, a very frequent subject in the Eastern Orthodox churches. The Stations of the Cross have become an integral part of the Roman Catholic cultus; other churches consider some of the fourteen incidents legendary and therefore do not use the "stations." Since the Protestant faith does not ascribe the function of intercession to Mary and the saints, it cannot admit works of art that emphasize it. (Many Protestants, failing to understand this point, are inclined to overlook it so long as the devotional atmosphere of the work appeals to them.) Needless to say, glorification in art of the institution and ritual of the Roman Catholic Church is unacceptable to the non-Roman churches.

A very considerable body of Christian art, from large wall paintings to minute book illuminations, was devoted to subjects that we now consider questionable or unacceptable. Still, the dominating themes have been Scriptural. They came mainly from the Old Testament books, Genesis, Exodus, the historical writings, Esther, Job, Jonah, and the apocryphal book Tobit; and from Christ's Nativity, baptism, Passion, death, resurrection, and ascension, from incidents related in The Acts of the Apostles and from The Revelation to John in the New Testament. To these must be added countless "portraits" of individual prophets, apostles, and saints. For liturgical and doctrinal reasons far less attention was given to Christ's active ministry. There are hundreds of representations of his Passion for every painting or sculpture dealing with his miracles of healing or his parables. It is by no means easy to find in older art convincing illustrations for some phases of

Christ's life, his relations to the people around him, or his teachings. (In this area Rembrandt's contribution is outstandingly helpful.)

Our far greater emphasis on the mission and message of the ever-living Christ opens new fields to the artist, beyond the comparatively narrow range of older Christian art, if he desires to help men and women experience the reality of Christ in a vital new encounter. He will find ample inspiration in the Gospels and Epistles to envisage Christ as challenging, strengthening, consoling, and most of all transforming personal and social life by the divine-human totality of his being.

Many other great themes close to the thinking of our time are waiting to be discovered. The prophetic teachings of the Old Testament had rarely been touched until the socially conscious painting of recent decades began to echo Amos' thunderings against those "who are at ease in Zion" and his demand, "Let justice roll down like waters, and righteousness like an everflowing stream" (Amos 6:1; 5:24). The church has every reason to be equally concerned with prophetic messages close to this spirit. Isaiah's magnificent vision of the time when swords will be beaten into plowshares, and "nation shall not lift up sword against nation, neither shall they learn war any more" (Isa. 2:4), expresses the undying hope of the millions, and calls out for inspired artists to place it before our eyes in compelling visual form.

Christian art of the Middle Ages and the Renaissance came no closer to an awareness of man's responsibility toward his fellow men than by showing the rich and the mighty, laymen as well as clergy, among the condemned sinners at the Last Judgment, or, more positively, when representing the seven acts of mercy: feeding the hungry, giving drink to the thirsty, welcoming strangers, clothing the naked, visiting the sick and those in prison, and burying the dead. As Christian art gives greater weight to the gospel of brotherly love, it can help us to realize that the individual's well-being, or, in religious terms, his redemption, is inextricably bound up with that of the community. By stressing in their art the "Social Gospel," the churches not only show their readiness to follow Christ's teaching but apply the basic truths that the natural and behavioral sciences have painstakingly rediscovered within the last few decades: that the health of individuals depends on their productive relationships with their social environment. When scientists stress the vital need for co-operation, they merely restate the command of brotherly love.

A critical survey of Christian art cannot, however, refer exclusively to problems of subject matter. Many works of art dealing with valid subjects are found wanting when judged by spiritual and aesthetic criteria. These would seem obvious, yet have been disregarded often enough to demand consideration. Respect for the subject inclines the viewer to overlook deficiencies that he would quickly spot in works of secular nature. Much has been tolerated or given recognition that is, in reality, cheap, tawdry, shoddy in craftsmanship, or that relies on slick handling of surface effects, on bathos and clever staging. We demand the whole truth, however painful it may be to contemplate. A Jesus praying in the Garden of Gethsemane with every strand of his hair beautifully smooth, every fold of his garments carefully arranged to make them look attractive, does not give a true image of the Savior in his darkest, most agonizing hour. Truth is not to be confused with an attempt to achieve historical accuracy. Delacroix once spoke of the "passion for accuracy that most people mistake for truth." It is a highly questionable ideal for Christian art and one that goes beyond the present state of archaeological knowledge. We cannot readily visualize the Palestine either of Old Testament times or as Jesus saw it, before the wars laid much of the country waste. In reality we have outgrown the insistence of a materialistic age on what was believed to be an exact reconstruction of the historical Jesus. Although recently there has been renewed interest in the effort to portray him historically as nearly as possible. Albert Schweitzer expressed the changed outlook of our age when he emphasized that Jesus as spiritually arisen within men is most significant for our time; " the spirit which goes forth from him and in the spirits of men strives for new influence and rule, is that which overcomes the world." [15]

D. Problems of Interpretation

Christian truth does not reside in externals but in the spirit of the artist's work. The questions to be asked are: Does it come close to the inner meaning of the Scriptural passage on which it is based? Has the artist fully understood its significance, and experienced it deeply enough himself to communicate it to us with directness and reverence? Christian art is no place for self-seeking or for casual amiability. The artist who looks across his shoulder to see if he pleases the crowd cannot create valid Christian art any more than his colleague to whom a Scriptural subject is just the pretext for a potboiler, a painting done simply to sell.

Examples of such " sins " against the spirit of Christian art are numerous, particularly during the periods of the Renaissance, the baroque, and the nineteenth century. Jacques Maritain rightly stated: " When in an art gallery we leave the rooms of the Primitives for those which display the glories of oil painting and a much more considerable material science, the foot advances over the floor but the soul sinks to the depths. It had been taking the air of the everlasting hills: it is now on the boards of a theater. . . . In the sixteenth century deceit installed itself in painting." [16] Such deceit becomes the more objectionable when the artist emphasizes sensuality. Nude figures, introduced because the subject demands them, should be treated with frankness and dignity in a mature way. One need not be prudish to find self-conscious presentation of nudity or provocative near-nudity thoroughly out of place in a work claiming to have a Christian message. Unfortunately, some pseudoreligious paintings and sculptures displaying a sprawling worldliness have gained wide popularity. Among them are several well-known canvases by Correggio and his

followers and that famous masterpiece of tongue-in-cheek insincerity, Batoni's *Repentant Magdalene*. What can give aesthetic delight to art lovers, or be of value to the art historian
as he traces the development of forms and of taste through
the centuries, does not necessarily communicate valid truth
to Christians of our generation. Such works belong by right
in private or public collections, not in the churches. In turn,
our time is ready once again to appreciate the great spiritual
and aesthetic qualities of periods and masters formerly little
regarded — Byzantine icons, early medieval art, Grünewald,
El Greco, Rembrandt, La Tour, Blake foremost among them.
Their work is closer to the aims of contemporary movements
in the arts as well as to the insights of modern theology. It
stands ready to take the place of what we have to discard.

To fulfill its high function as a servant of the Word, Christian art need not — and should not — be "preachy." Our age
has as strong a dislike for the unctuous in a work of art as in a
sermon. Even less admissible for permanent display in a
church are the artistic "fireworks" and eye-catching tricks
legitimate in secular art and in advertising, where they are
intended to attract and entertain the eye. People are too
familiar with the questionable sincerity of these devices not
to resent their introduction into the one place that so far has
withstood the onrush of commercialism. Love of God and
neighbor, like the gifts of the Spirit, cannot be "sold." They
grow naturally as the fruits of faith. The slightest admixture
of dishonesty, pretense, or vanity is unworthy of the church
and can discredit its message.

Christian art must likewise shun the overly elaborate and
overly decorative as well as affectation and artifice. They are
signs of weakness in a work of art, indicating a predominance
of form over content instead of the perfect harmony between
them that is the mark of the true masterpiece. Such "artiness"
makes Salvador Dali's religious paintings difficult to accept,
quite apart from the serious doubts awakened by his personality. He paints brilliantly, with an almost photographic real-

ism of detail. But his compositions are also replete with distracting elements of an arbitrary, farfetched nature. They treat the faith as a hothouse flower, not as man's spontaneous answer to God's free gift of grace. The symbol-starved public has welcomed them, although with the somewhat uneasy feeling of watching a prestidigitator perform because of their fascinating, almost eerie, effects. Besides, they demand less concentrated effort to be "read" than the far more challenging works of the expressionist or abstract painters.

Neither a mannered, effeminate style nor a display of sentimentality can produce valid Christian art. Sentimentality is a shallow attempt to parade a tearful emotionalism instead of the honest, if painful, revelation of truth. It blinds us to the real needs and demands of our human situation. "The first task, therefore, for those who would overcome the cleavage between Christianity and the arts," Amos Wilder has pointed out, "is to disassociate Christianity from some forms of sentimental art which obscure the issue and which distort the faith itself." [17] Practically every serious critic and theologian of our era, Protestant and Catholic alike, has condemned the sentimentality of the academic painters of the nineteenth century and the still more diluted offerings of commercial suppliers of "devotionals." Evelyn Underhill's defense of even "the crudest picture books of faith" as capable of giving inspiration to some persons overlooks the very real dangers inherent in this popular type of religious art.[18]

A Roman Catholic writer summed up the case in emphatic words: "Well might a man grow weak in faith and careless in practice who has been reared among spineless Madonnas, saccharine Sacred Hearts, swivel-hipped St. Josephs, and gaudily garbed Infants of Prague. . . . The yawn begins in childhood and the nausea comes in due time. If good people survive, lively of faith, in homes bedecked with these vulgar insults to the divine, that only proves anew how limitless is God's mercy and how mighty the power of his grace." [19] He could now add to this list clocks with religious images on their dials! In view of what we see in many a church and church school room, or on church bulletins, Protestants have little right to feel superior.

It can scarcely be denied that the image of the Savior himself has suffered most seriously from undue sentimentality. When the hierarchic, otherworldly vision of early medieval and Byzantine art gave way to the trend toward realism, artists were at liberty to create individualized portraits whose quality depended on their insight, ability, and taste. At once they were faced with the baffling problem of how to give a sense of both the divine and the human nature of Christ. Some of the early Flemish examples strike us today as entirely pedestrian. El Greco found his solution in a modified version of the Byzantine icon. Rembrandt chose to paint the Son of Man, though the depth of his colors and his supreme mastery of light and shadow powerfully suggest the mystery of the incarnation. The majority of artists, however, could give little or no indication of divinity except by an idealization that deprives Christ of the strength, no less than the weakness, of his humanity.

The task becomes almost insoluble when the subject is the transfiguration scene. Matthew's description of Jesus' appearance — "his face shone like the sun" (Matt. 17:2) — goes beyond anything human hands can do with brush and color. The theme has accordingly been rare in art, and the highly abstract and intensely serious Byzantine and Russian icons remain by far the most convincing versions. Raphael's highly extolled painting in the Vatican Gallery, completed after his early death by his pupil, Giulio Romano, leaves many a visitor more dismayed than inspired by the almost balletlike movements of the figures in the transfiguration scene. Moreover, Christ's manliness seems to dissolve into soft, feminine beauty accentuated by the swirling garments.

The concept of the beautiful Savior has remained dear to the multitudes ever since. Easy to look at, undemanding, the image became more and more attenuated until the Victorian period arrived at the "mild and meek" Jesus who calls us his own when we meet him walking in the garden. Any attentive reader of the New Testament must be struck by the one-sidedness and glaring inadequacy of this interpretation. Kierkegaard spoke up in sharp protest: "If the glory had been directly visible, so that everybody as a matter of course could see it, then it is false that Christ humbled himself and took upon him the form of a servant; it is superfluous to give warning against being offended, for how in the world could anybody be offended by glory attired in glory! And how in the world can it be explained that with Christ it fared as it did, that not everybody rushed up to see what was directly to be seen! No, there was 'nothing about him for the eye, no glamour that we should look upon him, no outward appearance that we should desire him' (Isa. 53:2); directly there was nothing to be seen but a lowly man who, by signs and wonders and by affirming that he was God, continually posited the possibility of offense." [20]

That memorable passage pronounces judgment upon the Hofmanns, Plockhorsts, Schmalzes, Bouguereaus, and their imitators, the great majority of the representations of Christ in the films, and the latest addition to the list of popular favorites, Warner Sallman's ubiquitous *Head of Christ*. Its immaculate grooming, high-gloss finish, and clever side lighting, familiar from the typical society photograph, make this picture the dream image of an utterly respectable Savior. Aloof from any entanglement in the troublesome business of daily life, he shows no awareness of the tragic depths of sin, guilt, and suffering from whence despairing souls cry out for help. He asks only for devotion, not for transformation. If many Christians have succumbed to the surface appeal of this portrait, it may be because they often know Christ only from a few isolated, appealing quotations and parables. Surely this is not the humble, yet at the same time insistently demanding, preacher who had to say of himself, as he walked the dusty roads, "Foxes have holes, and birds of the air have nests, but

the Son of man has nowhere to lay his head" (Luke 9:58).
Seen against the background of the whole gospel, the picture
is deficient, or actually misleading. With the best intentions
Warner Sallman has changed the bread of life into frosted
cake.

Admittedly, the problem of how to present Christ in his
full stature to our generation is difficult and will tax the powers
of the greatest artists. If they defer to custom and tradition,
everyone may at once recognize the figure; if they try to create
a new image, people may at first be baffled. Yet our time does
see Christ in new and different ways; last century's conception
is no longer vital enough to stir modern minds. It is too feminine, too pale, to answer to our needs. The proliferation of
the inadequate image is one reason why many thoughtful
persons have turned away from the churches in disappoint-
ment. We cannot abandon it soon enough.

But what are we to put in its place? Jesus Christ has many
faces: he is the very human, loving servant of all, the forgiving
friend of outcasts and sinners, as well as the determined
prophet who lashed out against self-righteousness and lack of
social responsibility, who would not accept the rich young
man as a disciple unless he first gave his possessions to the
poor, and who chased money-changers and traders from the
Temple. He is the eternal Son, created before the beginning
of the world, the high priest of the infinite God, the just judge
who will pronounce judgment at the end of the age; and at
the same time the lonely, broken sufferer giving his own life
that others may be saved. No wonder Paul exults in contemplation of the "riches of his grace" (Eph. 1:7).

To combine all these aspects of Christ in one image is obviously impossible. The artist has to make a choice that will
be confession of his own faith if it is to be convincing. He must,
as it were, build from within himself with absolute faithful-
ness to the image in his own heart. If he cannot do so — either
because this inner image is not clear enough, or because he is
afraid of adverse criticism — he should, in fairness to himself

and others, abstain from the attempt, as Rembrandt did for many years or as Manessier has done in our time.

The Christian artist must guard against any tendency to extol any specific group, race, or nation. It is natural that every group should want to see Christ as one of its own, for he belongs to all mankind. He is brother to all, just as his gospel must be preached to every nation. Negro and Oriental artists are on solid ground when they show him with the features of their people, and they deserve encouragement. Nobody seems to have thought it strange that he should have been portrayed, through these many centuries, as a man of the Western world, in disregard of the given circumstances of his life on earth. Racial characteristics, however, best remain incidental and should not obtrude themselves. When will our mission schools realize how ill-advised it is to show a blond, "nordic" image of Christ to dark-skinned people? Instead of coming close to them, he must remain a stranger. Far better the perhaps artless, but direct and personal, work of a local painter or craftsman than such importations.

Equally to be shunned is a show of elegance. Jesus was not a member of the upper classes. He worked with his hands prior to his ministry and moved among the outcasts of society. His sympathies were always with the workers. The task of art in the church is not to make faith glamorous or "attractive," but to deepen and strengthen it by helping to change self-seeking into concern for others, passive reception of the message into active commitment. The essential difference is between those who see in Christianity a glorification of what they imagine they are, a wish-fulfillment to enhance their self-image, and who therefore desire to see only a beautiful Mary, an elegant and appealing Jesus, and those who see in Christianity the denial of our materialistic values, the scandal, the stone of stumbling, the truth about ourselves that, once we accept it, leads to rebirth, to becoming what we were meant to be.

Another serious problem is the representation of the crucified Christ. During the last century a strong current of opposition made itself felt. The German poet Theodor Storm, a dedicated Christian himself, sharply attacked the perpetuation of what he called the horror image of unforgivingness. Some Christians today agree with this view. They are repelled by the cruelty of the scene and believe it can obscure faith in the ever-living Christ. The churches, they feel, should concentrate their emphasis on Easter, not on Good Friday. Long ago John Donne already answered these objections:

> Since Christ embrac'd the crosse itself, dare I
> His image, th' image of the crosse deny? . . .
> Who from the picture would avert his eye,
> How could he flye his paines, who there did dye?

And Christina Rossetti asked, in a similar vein:

> Shall Christ hang on the cross, and we not look? . . .
> Cry shame upon us! For he bore our shame
> In agony, and we look on at ease
> With neither hearts on flame nor cheeks on flame.

The two opposed views are hard to reconcile. Too much preoccupation with the physical sufferings of the Savior can become a morbid obsession; refusal to face them frankly can betray an overoptimistic understanding of the meaning of the cross. We cannot forget Paul's clear-cut decision: "We preach Christ crucified, a stumbling-block to Jews and folly to Gentiles, but to those who are called, both Jews and Greeks, Christ the power of God and the wisdom of God" (I Cor. 1:23–24).

May not our almost frantic fear of death motivate some of the objections against the representation in art of the crucifixion? Death surrounds us everywhere, riding the highways, flickering daily in many forms across the television screen, staring at us from the headlines in the newspapers. Yet we shrink from using the hated word if we can possibly avoid it, and use all kinds of euphemisms if we cannot. We embalm our dead to make them look attractive, and have sometimes developed elaborate funereal rituals far removed from the joyful faith of the early Christians in the resurrection of the body and eternal life. Strong in this faith, they looked upon the day of death as the true birthday in Christ. Our age ranks the physician who prolongs the life of the body far higher, in terms of rewards, than the minister who cares for the life of the soul, or the teacher who gives wings to the mind. The skeleton, once a powerful symbol of the shortness of man's days, freely used as a reminder that we must be prepared to meet our Maker, has sunk to the lowly estate of a Halloween joke, so that we may laugh at it. This fear of death points to the weakness of the faith of many professed Christians.

Artists of our time have reacted sharply against the hedonistic, if not cowardly, refusal to admit the reality of death. Their emphatic insistence on making us face the truth has led to the deeply disturbing crucifixion scenes of recent years. In them the whole creation is seen groaning in travail and crying out, with Christ, "My God, my God, why hast thou forsaken me?"

Such frankness is sorely needed to penetrate the screens we build up around us in order to escape confrontation with the ultimate problem of all existence. But if this witness of contemporary art is valid, it is also one-sided. The cross, D. M. Baillie has stated, was the worst thing that had ever happened through the sin of men but likewise the best that had ever happened in the providence of God.[21] The two aspects have resulted in two distinct versions of the crucifixion scene in art. One emphasizes the heart-rending agony of the Savior; the other shows him heroically bearing his sufferings, asking God to forgive his enemies "for they know not what they do." It also reminds us of Christ's dying words, "Father, into thy hands I commit my spirit." The deepest interpretation will communicate to us the assurance that nothing whatever can "separate us from the love of God in Christ Jesus our Lord" (Rom. 8:39). This assurance is the supreme message of the

Christian faith, the unshakable rock on which it is founded. Under its sign the cross became the means of redemption; its very paradox fulfills Jesus' promise that the sorrow of those who love him will turn into joy. (John 16:20.)

The Gospels teach neither a joyless faith nor one that tries to bypass the cross. Precisely, the recognition and acceptance of the dichotomy of joy and sorrow, death and resurrection, enables the Christian faith to speak the truth about life. The Christian artist's task is therefore twofold. He must communicate to his generation that Christ, in Pascal's word, " will be in agony until the end of the world," and that he reigns even now in glory as Lord and Judge of the world. The twofold verity found expression in the deeply serious, yet at the same time triumphant " Christ in Majesty " of the early Middle Ages and the " Pantocrator " of the Byzantine churches. The creative artists of our time are finding their way back to this great affirmation without slavishly copying earlier models. They no longer strive for the physical beauty that had become the bane of Christian art when it degenerated into mere prettiness. Their aim is spiritual beauty, the only beauty worthy of the faith, a " radiance of the invisible within the visible." Physical beauty, when employed in works of Christian art, should be no more than a veil through which the divinity of the soul can shine, Friedrich von Schlegel wrote a century and a half ago. Yet the radiance of the spirit can never be self-evident and unendangered in Christian art, for it is wrested from sin through grace, and granted through redemption. The incarnation stands under the tension of Good Friday and Easter, and the formal aspect of Christian art must mirror the same tension. " This can hardly be suggested by a smooth classicism of undisturbed harmony which easily becomes superficial, lifeless, and empty because it fails to meet our situation. For a Christian art truly born out of the incarnation, the divine radiance can only become visible in what is human when the latter dies with Christ and rises again in Christ. . . . Strength and depth of Christian art depend on how far it gains hold of the incarnation (with all its radiations) even in the creative imagination." [22]

Christian joy, then, is like a smile through tears, like the rainbow after the storm. Children's joy is like that. They accept the closeness of happiness and sorrow unquestioningly. When we grow older we prefer to suppress the knowledge that the two are inseparably linked. We strive with might and main for pure joy undimmed by the shadow of sorrow, only to be disappointed again and again. The creative artist knows from his own experience the true nature of joy. He also knows that beauty stands under the same law because it is joy made visual, a gift of grace, not the property of material forms.

> " Only who has lifted the lyre
> among shadows, too,
> may divining render
> the infinite praise.
> Only who with the dead has eaten
> of the poppy that is theirs,
> will never again lose
> the most delicate tone." [23]

To do justice to the dichotomy of the Christian faith, the artist must have gone through a spiritual Anastasis, a descent into the depths and a rising from them. But his work should not carry his knowledge of the depths as a heavy burden. There is nothing commendable or Christian about gloom. Truth does not require draping in black, or an insistent harping on pain and disharmony. The truth of the Christian message is the truth of grace, of God's infinite love despite man's unworthiness, and of our living in Christ despite sorrow and death. The artist may feel the need to shock us and dispel our illusions by the harshness of his forms, but he is in the truest sense Christian only when he works from love, not hatred. To paraphrase Paul's words: If he has prophetic powers, and understands all mysteries and all knowledge, and has all faith, so as to remove mountains, but has no love, he is nothing (I Cor. 13:2).

When the person of the Savior or a particular passage in the Scriptures has become so meaningful to an artist as to awaken in him the compelling urge for expression, he will strive for the most convincing artistic realization. His work must be able to stand on its own merit in the eyes of unbelievers as well as of believers. Pious intentions are not enough. As Dorothy Sayers said, "Not Herod, not Caiaphas, not Pilate, not Judas, ever contrived to fasten upon Jesus Christ the reproach of insipidity; that final indignity was left for pious hands to inflict." [24] Not that we have the right to expect every artist to be a genius of the highest order. We can gladly accept the sincere offerings of less highly endowed artists — provided they speak with absolute honesty and do not try to say more than they have felt or experienced themselves. The halting, unpolished speech of a man who has a vision of truth that he conveys to us with such power as to open our eyes to it has far higher value than the eloquence of an orator who enjoys his own brilliancy. Kierkegaard expressed this perfectly when he wrote: "In a devotional sense, to be eloquent is a mere frill in the same way that to be beautiful is a happy privilege, but is still a nonessential frill. In a devotional sense, earnestness: to listen in order to act, this is the highest thing of all, and, God be praised, every man is capable of it if he so wills." [25]

Christian art, by reason of its high purpose, demands if anything a more, not less, critical attitude than secular art. While encouraging every honest effort, we must be uncompromising in our refusal to sanction what is pretentious, self-seeking, or insipid. Father M. A. Couturier, the builder of the great church at Assy, France, and a pioneer of modern Christian art, explained why he brought in the best-living artists: "We were tired of always seeing in our churches the most mediocre examples of painting and sculpture. In the long run, we thought, this mediocrity could only result in seriously altering the religious psychology of clergy and worshipers alike. We were also aware that unbelievers, comparing these works to the great Christian art of the past, would inevitably question the vitality of a Faith and a Church that could remain content with them." [26]

The church of Christ has the right and the duty to set highest aesthetic and spiritual standards for Christian art. What matters is that the artist come close to the ultimate verities of the faith. When he has seen the truth and spoken it directly and reverently, we shall be rewarded by new and deeper understanding and inspired to greater love of God if our eyes and hearts are open to his message. Unless the soil is prepared, the good seed cannot grow and ripen.

Chapter V

The Task

of the Churches

> *One cannot doubt that one reason for the*
> *alienation between the Protestant churches*
> *and the artists is the fact that the church*
> *has been for so long a bad consumer, an*
> *undiscriminating patron.*
> — Truman B. Douglass.

To see signs of a rebirth of Christian art in our time runs counter to the frequently heard assertion that there is no longer any vital relationship between the visual arts and the faith. Outside observers have pointed to the comparative scarcity of contemporary work of religious nature as proof that the churches have no message capable of inspiring creative minds. Churchmen, inclined to deplore what to them are incomprehensible new forms of art, blame the rift on the secularism of an age that willfully, and to its peril, turns deaf ears to the word of God.

Neither of these views contains the whole truth. Artists as a group are among those least affected in their thinking by the materialistic outlook of our society, whether they feel compelled to expose the evils they see rampant everywhere or believe in letting their work quietly testify to the ongoing life of the spirit. " By maintaining his loyalty to the value of art — to responsible creative work, the search for perfection, the sensitiveness to quality — the artist is one of the most moral and idealistic of beings, although his influence on practical affairs may seem very small." [1] The predominance of secular work in galleries and exhibitions of contemporary art is in part explained by the fact that paintings and sculptures made for specific churches are rarely shown publicly prior to being installed. Many artists would be happy to serve the churches of Christ to the best of their ability, but they cannot do so unless they are granted the freedom of expressing themselves in forms that are alive and meaningful to them. This is their truth, and a compromise with the prevailing taste for the innocuous or an imitation of the past would be a betrayal of their convictions. But when an artist has the disappointing, if not humiliating, experience of finding his religious work ignored or sharply rebuffed by the churches, he may decide that he has to avoid Christian themes altogether if he wants to earn his livelihood.

This lack of response is one of the lingering effects of the withdrawal of the churches from the mainstream of culture that became apparent in the eighteenth century. As they encapsuled themselves within their own structures, they lost touch with the creative forces in every field of human endeavor, their influence dwindled, and their message meant less and less to adventurous minds moving forward to revolutionary discoveries. Slowly, and not without strong opposition, the major denominations gave up their isolation when the "Social Gospel" raised its challenge. Selfish interests were quick to sense a potential enemy and demanded that the churches should "stay out" of politics, business, industry, and the problems of the social life — as if anything vitally affecting God's children *could* remain outside their concern. We have seen dedicated Christian leaders defamed as "subversive," forced out of their pulpits, physically attacked and jailed. Sometimes the intimidation was successful, but every defeat seems to have produced greater determination. Today the churches know that the world expects them to take a stand on controversial issues, and that courageous pronouncements and actions in the spirit of the gospel win more souls for Christ than fence-straddling half-measures.

To understand their reluctance to take a similar active in-

terest in cultural endeavors is the more difficult as the obsta-
cles are nowhere nearly so imposing. No artists of standing
have advocated that the churches should leave their province
strictly alone. On the contrary, everyone is eager for them to
become involved, and not merely when the questions of mor-
ality and censorship arise. Most churchmen would probably
agree with H. Richard Niebuhr's statement that " the world of
culture — man's achievement — exists within the world of grace
— God's Kingdom." [2] But to bear fruit this insight must be
followed up energetically.

An auspicious beginning was made a few years ago with
the establishment by the National Council of Churches of a
Department of Worship and the Arts. It has functioned since
1954 through commissions on architecture, art, music, drama,
literature, and ways of worship, with dedicated leadership and
the enthusiastic co-operation of distinguished representatives
of the various fields. Unfortunately, however, its work has
been greatly hampered by the lack of sufficient funds. Without adequate support it cannot achieve its aim to offer a much-
needed meeting ground for faith and the culture of our time.
Most of the projects it started could not be developed despite
mounting evidence of interest on the part of ministers, congregations, and students, who sent in a stream of requests for
help and advice.

Until the Department of Worship and the Arts is substantially strengthened, the denominations traditionally favorable
to the visual arts may have to proceed independently. It was
heartening to read a resolution adopted by the Anglican bish-
ops at their Lambeth Conference of 1958: " The Conference
believes that the presentation of the message of the Bible to
the world requires great sensitiveness to the outlook of the people of today, and urges that imaginative use be made of all the
resources of literature, art, music, and drama, and of new
techniques appealing to eye as well as to ear." Everyone concerned about bringing the arts and the Christian faith closer
together will rejoice at this affirmation and hope it may not

only be followed by similar ones from other denominations but also be implemented by positive steps.

Since what is primarily required at this stage is informed leadership, we must look to the divinity schools to provide it. Most of them have already expanded their program to include courses in literature and music as they relate to the faith, but so far little has been done for the visual arts. These are still being bypassed, very few schools having made definite provision for their proper study. The main reason usually given is the chronic state of poverty of the institutions where the nation's future ministers and religious educators are being trained. It would be a worthy task for some of the great foundations interested in fostering the arts, and for our leading art collectors, to endow a chair or help establish a Center of Christian art, especially as the cost would be considerably below the price of a single old-master painting. Another reason sometimes given is the heavy load of required courses in the schools of theology. Yet experience has shown that elective courses in art history and appreciation are well attended because many ministerial students are conscious of their need for a thorough grounding in it.

Centers or institutes of Christian art have done pioneer work in research and training at several European universities, but none as yet exists in our country, with its millions of Protestant church members and its amply financed scientific and technological institutions. The aim would not be so much to train specialists — although some students may wish to make Christian art their major field of concentration — or to compete with professional art schools, as to provide prospective ministers and Christian educators with a scholarly introduction to the riches as well as the problems of Christian art, past and present. The emphasis should be on developing discriminating understanding, on breaking down barriers of ignorance and prejudice. A warm, informed enthusiasm rather than a superficial acquaintance with facts and names will widen the horizon of the student and enrich his personal life so that he or she can in turn enrich others through preaching, teaching, and by example.

The historical course would touch at many points on the backgrounds of Biblical history, particularly in the study of Egyptian, Babylonian and Assyrian art. Later it would help bring to fuller life the study of the early Christian, medieval, and Reformation periods. The gradual unfolding of modern styles in their organic development would dispel the false stigma of arbitrariness attached to them by the uninformed. Such a course naturally could only lay a foundation. It would prove its worth if it established in the student a lasting relationship to the spiritual ground of art in its divers manifestations and an open-minded receptiveness to the creative efforts of all ages, including his own. Other courses could deal specifically with Christian symbolism and iconography, and the problems of how to use the arts in Christian preaching and teaching.

A Center of Christian art could also reach out to the men and women already at work in the churches. There is a pressing need for more extension courses, conferences, summer school sessions and workshops. A Center of Christian art would be expected to prepare publications of both a scholarly and a practical nature, gather and distribute information about teaching aids, slides, filmstrips, good reproductions, and books. It would become a clearinghouse for artists and architects capable of serving the needs of the churches, and help bridge the gulf between creators and prospective clients. The opportunities for productive work would seem to be almost unlimited and would benefit all denominations, not just the one under whose auspices the Center would be founded. Christian art cannot be split up into sectarian divisions; it is in the highest sense ecumenical.

There is no reason to fear that such efforts would overly stress the aesthetic realm to the detriment of social action, evangelism, mission, or other fields where the churches are vitally involved. These would rather be strengthened if some of the lukewarm and nominal church members could be brought to a new commitment to the Christian life through the medium of the aesthetic experience. Truman B. Douglass recently reminded the churches, after sharply taking them to task for their apathy in the field of the arts, that "what is at stake here is not merely good taste but truth. The serious artist is only secondarily concerned with beauty in the aesthetic and formal sense. His primary engagement is with reality. This is also, if they know their calling, the objective of the theologian and every committed Christian. The artists can be bearers of truth to the Christian community if that community is humble and open in its conversation with them." [2]

Once the theological schools accept their responsibility for the training of the younger generation in the field of art, we can expect to get the informed leadership that is now largely unavailable. In the meantime, church workers and pastors are left to their own initiative. If they wish to make up for what they were not offered at their theological schools, they will find the art department of the nearest college, the division of education of a museum, or a local art teacher or supervisor glad to arrange for conferences. It is virtually impossible to imagine a city or town of any size where a qualified person would not be available for guidance and instruction. Men and women who love the arts have an almost evangelistic zeal to open the doors of appreciation to others.

Informal meetings of this sort might lead to the development of a more general adult education program by a church or group of churches, perhaps along the lines of the "University of Life" idea. Many church organizations find themselves from time to time in danger of lapsing into routine; a new idea can be of great value. Members who had been wondering about the meaning and origin of the numerous symbols in their house of worship might welcome an opportunity to learn about them. Any purposeful study of a particular topic related to art and the faith, if done under expert direction, is likely to draw in passive members, attract newcomers, and — still more important — lead to renewed Bible-reading.

A number of churches have achieved good results by arranging exhibitions of original works of art (or selected good reproductions). The Church of the Restoration (Universalist-Unitarian) of Mt. Airy, Philadelphia, Pennsylvania, for instance, has converted a lounge into a gallery where it presents the work of local and regional artists to its members and friends. The project has aroused keen interest among church people and artists, is well publicized, and may grow into a new cultural center for its neighborhood.

Efforts of this kind can have particular value for new suburban developments. These vast "bedroom towns" are too distant from the downtown area of the metropolis to which they technically belong to permit regular use of its diversified facilities (museums, theaters, concerts, lectures, and so forth), and too young to have a distinct sense of community. They are in serious danger of becoming cultural deserts unless the churches recognize their responsibilities — and opportunities — in the changing pattern of American life.

An ambitious nationwide "Church Art Today" exhibit was organized by Grace Cathedral (Episcopal) of San Francisco for the purpose of "stimulating the production of good contemporary religious art and promoting its commissioning and purchase by churches and individuals." Held for the second time in the spring of 1960, it received more than six hundred entries from all parts of the United States. An art exhibit was also one of the features of the "Festival of Religious Art" held in 1959 at First Church (Congregational) in Cambridge, Massachusetts, under the title "Man's Search for Meaning." Sessions were devoted to religious drama, music (special attention was given to jazz), and the dance. The exceptional attendance clearly indicated keen interest on the part of the community. These are just a few examples of positive action.

The churches have also every reason to welcome exhibitions of religious art prepared, largely for their benefit, by museums in numerous communities. In addition, almost every museum is now celebrating the great feast days of the faith with special exhibits, and several are providing Christmas and Easter cards reproducing appropriate works of Christian art. The Metropolitan Museum and the Morgan Library in New York in particular — but others as well — deserve credit for making available a variety of reasonably priced religious greeting cards, a service still largely unfamiliar to church people.

Some churches have begun to collect examples of Christian arts and crafts as aids in religious education. The Charles Street Meeting House (Universalist) in Boston has brought together a remarkable group of sculptures, paintings, textiles, and small devotional objects illustrating the major religions of the world, from primitive fetishes and pre-Columbian carvings to Buddhist bronzes and temple hangings. Such a collection is invaluable for the study of non-Christian forms of faith. Many a church school could arrange a similar display, if on a smaller scale. Private collectors and public museums are usually willing to lend works of art to churches for temporary display. Church-related colleges and schools have the same opportunities, and the interest generated by a series of loan exhibitions may in the end lead to a permanent collection.

Any sign of active interest in the heritage of Christian art is welcome. The majority of our people are still very little aware of it. One often hears the question, after showing a group of slides to a church audience: " Why have we never seen these beautiful and inspiring works before? We had no idea they existed." But we must guard against looking backward only. The paramount duty of the churches is to the living. It is more difficult to fulfill because we can never be certain if we read the signs of the times correctly; it is also more " controversial " and therefore frightens the faint of heart. Difficulties and uncertainties, however, ought not to deter the churches from speaking the word of salvation here and now, and to the creative men and women in our midst as well. They need to feel at home in the church of Christ instead of being treated as errant children.

We cannot expect to have great Christian art by sitting back and complaining about its scarcity. Art does not grow in a vacuum; it needs to be nourished like any young plant. The churches are entitled to make demands of the artist who is willing to serve them, but in return he can ask of them a greater openness to his new forms and insights than they have generally shown in the past, and a deeper respect for sincere, solid craftsmanship devoid of false glamour and affected pose. The growth of a vigorous contemporary Christian art in Europe was mainly the result of the practice of the churches to allot a definite percentage of their building funds to the purchase of works of art, and their readiness to accept courageous new solutions. In order to keep independent artists and craftsmen productively occupied and prevent their drifting into secular work, they also have been given many large and small commissions for which we habitually turn to commercial firms, such as for altar furnishings, communion vessels, lecterns, baptismal fonts, posters, bulletins, certificates and documents of all sorts. We could easily adopt similar measures, since there is ample talent among our own artists. But a valid Christian art must be built on a broad basis, and to encourage it we shall have to abandon our tendency to go only after "big" names.

Neither should we forget the field of the graphic arts. They offer major opportunities for Christian artists to find an interested public once churches and laymen realize that an original print, be it an etching, woodcut, silk-screen print or serigraph, produced in a small edition and signed by the artist, can generally be bought for twenty-five dollars or less. Few church members are aware of the existence of these prints, or know where to buy them. Yet private art dealers' galleries have multiplied within the last decade and are now found in every major city. No interested layman or minister should hesitate to visit them; he will be welcome to browse and ask questions and will not be pressured into buying. These galleries are the normal outlets for independent artists. Any church desiring to exhibit contemporary graphic art will find them ready to do everything they can to help. Everyone familiar with the outstanding work being done by numerous artists in this field must wish for better communication between them and the churches. Great possibilities to encourage Christian art and at the same time deepen the spiritual life of the churches and their members are lost because creators and audience have not been brought together. Few families are unable to afford an original print; few church school budgets too small to afford some for their worship centers or classrooms to replace the omnipresent, mechanically reproduced standard offerings of the commercial suppliers that we have seen far too often.

An important, though still widely neglected, task for creative artists is the illustration of printed church school curricular materials, church programs, calendars, bulletins, journals, and magazines. Illustrations present special problems; their quality has ranged from the excellent to the atrocious. Many artists of the highest rank have produced outstanding examples. Some, like Schnorr von Carolsfeld and William Morris, did their best work as illustrators; others have made illustration their main specialty, although some, in particular Alexandre Bida and James Tissot, have been so absorbed by the minutiae of supposedly historical detail as to lose sight of the essential aspects of the message.

To prepare a good illustration the artist must be a man of skill and taste, well versed in a wide range of techniques and able to choose what is most appropriate in a given case. He must understand the deeper significance of the text, especially when it is taken from the Bible, and must strive to reveal, with strength and clarity, the spiritual truth of a scene over and above its vivid setting. He must be willing to subordinate himself to the text instead of interpreting it freely as is the right of the artist working independently. His gravest danger is the temptation to prettify, poetize, or overdramatize. False pathos and sentimentality are as much to be avoided as all theatrical effects.

Great efforts have lately been made to popularize the so-called comic-strip technique for religious illustrations meant for children. It is claimed that our young people are used to it and that it may awaken their interest in the Scriptures. But by imitating the hectic pace and the thrill-a-minute presentation of the typical comics it actually changes the Biblical stories until they can scarcely be recognized, cheapening and degrading them in the process. The whole concept is a thoroughly objectionable, bad means to a good end, besides being quite useless. Any child persuaded to read the Bible in the expectation of finding it " exciting " will quickly discover how much he has been deceived. The cheaply produced, crude fabrications with their garish colors and absurd designs should be rejected by the churches. Let us make a greater effort to instill in our children respect for the Bible as the record of God's revelation to man, a book too lofty and serious to suffer the ignominy of being exploited for a series of pulp comics.

Other possibilities for assignments that could go to artists are the covers of our Sunday bulletins or calendars. Too often they are mass-produced and show either pretty color photos of the kind we see in magazines and travel brochures (" The frost is on the punkin," " Winter-Wonderland," and so forth) or reproductions of devotional pictures of the all-too-familiar kind. Several new series, either with symbolic designs or original graphic art, exemplify that these covers can be real sources of inspiration. Could not the larger churches with their membership of several thousands commission their own covers, at least for the major holiday services? The cost would be scarcely more than what they are already paying, and the opportunity for bringing art and the faith together would not go by default. In defense of the commercial supply houses, it should be said that most of them would probably be willing to improve the quality of their stock if they could count on satisfactory response, though this does not relieve them of their responsibility, as servants of the churches, to be in the lead instead of dragging behind. Among the products most urgently in need of drastic change are the wall calendars offered free to the churches by various firms and establishments, with their annual repetition of the same hackneyed assortment of the very weakest " devotional " art.

Many churches look to their denominational boards and councils to offer leadership in the reconciliation between art and faith. They could set an example, if they became fully aware of their opportunities, from the building and furnishing of their headquarters to the design of brochures, reports, educational materials, and attendance charts. Even those pins, once frequently given to children as attendance awards, were usually worthless from an artistic and inspirational point of view!

When we are thinking of improving a church school room or youth chapel, we may well call on the young people themselves to apply their talents for artistic expression. It is easy to get willing young hands to work together on a mural or mosaic, and projects of this sort can have great spiritual value. The selection of the subject, the research needed for the design, are bound to lead students and teachers deeply into aspects of the faith that they might otherwise have never touched. If a trained person can act as leader, he or she will have the wholehearted co-operation of the children. Within a few months a nondescript room may change into a place dear to the children because it is their very own. A similar co-operative effort could do much for institutional chapels at state hospitals, rehabilitation centers, reform schools, and penitentiaries. To take an active part in such work can bring far-reaching spiritual benefit to patients and inmates.

We would be shortsighted, indeed, were we to despise the self-taught amateur in the arts. Many a small country church that now stands bare and depressingly impersonal could profit from the sincere, straightforward work of a gifted " Sunday " painter who is modest enough to know his limitations and does not simply try to copy some well-known model. The true " primitive " artist in fact usually creates in a style much closer to modern than to academic art, as the remarkable development of an authentic indigenous Christian art in Haiti has again shown. Folk painting disappeared shamefacedly when the chromo came in during the last century. Today we appreciate its unsophisticated charm. If we encourage the signs of genuine new growth, we might see a revival of it.

The widespread interest in handicrafts, together with the desire of many older people to take up creative hobbies, opens another field where alert churches can stimulate fruitful activity. Many of the men who are now making fine carpentry their avocation would gladly contribute their skills to a gradual refurnishing of their church building. A hand-wrought altar or Communion table, lectern, organ housing, hymn indicator, or new lighting fixture will much improve the worshipful atmosphere of the church. Some talented women might design an altar cloth, a hooked rug, or embroidered panel with a religious motif. While such projects require inspiring and at the same time tactful leadership to prevent self-consciousness and vanity from entering, they will link each participant closer to the faith and to the community of believers if all follow the apostle's admonition: "Whatever your task, work heartily, as serving the Lord and not men" (Col. 3:23).

In his thoughtful book entitled *Contrasts: The Arts and Religion,* Alec Robertson quotes a word of Van Gogh's: "To try to understand the real significance of what the great artists, the serious masters, tell us in their masterpieces, *that* leads to God." He then continues:

> I am convinced, by experience, that Van Gogh is expressing, in those words, what the majority of the seriously minded among the younger generation feel instinctively or think consciously today. Few of them go to church, but they do listen to music, read poetry, look at pictures; and they pass from a world of opposed political and religious creeds and dogmas into a world far more spiritual and harmonious. It is therefore very understandable that for so many of the younger generation art has taken the place of religion, and perhaps it will be

art's revenge at the indifference which religion has displayed
to it since the Renaissance that through the work of the artist,
rather than the labors of the priest, men will return to religion.[4]

No doubt this is overstating the case, but the churches cannot lightly dismiss the element of truth in it. Indeed, almost
everywhere indications of a changing attitude are apparent,
both toward the arts as such and toward Christian art in particular. All disappointments and failures notwithstanding, we
can rejoice at the many outspokenly contemporary new
churches with their clarity and simplicity, their absence of
pomp and empty show, their insistence on truth. Creative artists are giving to the faith works of challenging, inspiring character — and beauty. This new art renounces richness in forms
and materials. It is sparse, austere, filled with awe before the
Almighty as befits an age that does not yet know whether it
is destined to be the last before Armageddon. Because the fearful predicament of our existential situation has shattered smug-
ness and complacency, we are ready to confess our total dependence on grace, and sense that the artist expresses our
truth when his work cries out, " I believe; help my unbelief! "

Will the friendlier climate within our churches lead to a
Christian art of lasting greatness and to a deeper spirituality?
We cannot tell, nor should we worry about it. All we can do
is open the doors of the church of Christ to the artist as a " fellow workman for God," in humble recognition that "neither he
who plants nor he who waters is anything, but only God who
gives the growth " (I Cor. 3:7).

Notes

Chapter I. Spiritual Foundations of the Arts

1. Jacques Maritain and Jean Cocteau, *Art and Faith: Letters* (Philosophical Library, Inc., 1948), pp. 97 f.

2. Ralph Waldo Emerson, *Society and Solitude* (Houghton Mifflin Company, 1904), p. 48.

3. Nicolas Berdyaev, *The Beginning and the End* (Torchbooks, Harper & Brothers, 1957), pp. 174 ff.

4. Henri Focillon, *Hokousai* (Paris, 1925), pp. 95 f.

5. Ernst Cassirer, *An Essay on Man* (Anchor Books, Doubleday & Company, Inc., 1953), p. 210.

6. John Dewey, *Art as Experience* (Minton, Balch & Company, 1934), p. 66.

7. Robert Goldwater and Marco Treves (eds.), *Artists on Art* (Pantheon Books, Inc., 1945), pp. 384, 447 f.

8. Frederick Ward Kates, *The Use of Life* (Harper & Brothers, 1953), pp. 38 f.

9. William Barrett, *Irrational Man* (Doubleday & Co., Inc., 1958), pp. 40, 57.

Chapter II. Our Heritage

1. C. Kraehling, *The Synagogue* (Yale University Press, 1956).

2. Walter Elliger, *Zur Entstehung und frühen Entwicklung der altchristlichen Bildkunst* (Dieterich, Leipzig, 1934), pp. 34 f., 110.

3. Otto Von Simson, *Sacred Fortress* (University of Chicago Press, 1948), pp. 80, 98.

4. Hans Freiherr von Campenhausen, " Die Bilderfrage als theologisches Problem der alten Kirche," *Das Gottesbild im Abendland.* (Eckart-Verlag, Witten und Berlin, 1957), p. 97.

5. Louis Bréhier, *L'Art Chrétien* (Paris, 1928), p. 85.

6. Kenneth Scott Latourette, *A History of Christianity* (Harper & Brothers, 1953), p. 525.

7. Emile Mâle, *Religious Art from the Twelfth to the Eighteenth Century* (Pantheon Books, Inc., 1949), pp. 64 f.

8. Elizabeth Gilmore Holt, *Literary Sources of Art History* (Princeton University Press, 1947), pp. 18 f.

9. Adolf Katzenellenbogen, "*The Central Tympanum* at Vézelay," *Art Bulletin*, Vol. XXVI (1944), p. 146.

10. Hans Carl von Haebler, *Das Bild in der evangelischen Kirche* (Evangelische Verlagsanstalt, Berlin, 1957), p. 13.

11. Henry Beveridge (ed.), *Institutes of the Christian Religion* (Edinburgh, 1845), Vol. I, pp. 92, 98, 100 (sections 2, 9, 12).

12. Thomas à Kempis, *Imitation of Christ* (Modern Library, Inc.; Random House, Inc., 1943), p. 317.

13. Fernanda Wittgens, "*Leonardo's Last Supper* Resurrected," *Art News*, Annual Christmas Edition (1955), p. 52.

14. Erwin Panofsky, *The Life and Art of Albrecht Dürer* (Princeton University Press, 1955), pp. 198 f.

15. *Ibid.*, pp. 222 f.

16. Walter Friedlaender, *Caravaggio-Studies* (Princeton University Press, 1953), p. 120.

17. Haebler, *op. cit.*, p. 41.

18. Wilhelm Reinhold Valentiner, *Rembrandt and Spinoza* (Phaidon Press, Ltd., London, 1957), p. 57.

19. W. A. Visser 't Hooft, *Rembrandt and the Gospel* (The Westminster Press, 1957), pp. 70, 19.

20. Paul Romaine-Musculus, "L'Église Réformée et l'Art," *Problèmes de l'Art Sacré*, ed. Victor-Henri Debidour (Le Nouveau Portique, Paris, 1951), p. 102.

21. Hanns Lilje, *The Valley of the Shadow*, tr. by Olive Wyon (Muhlenberg Press, 1950), p. 91.

Chapter III. The Function of Christian Art

1. Gilbert Cope, *Symbolism in the Bible and the Church* (Philosophical Library, Inc., 1959), p. 49.

2. T. S. Eliot, *The Complete Poems and Plays, 1909–1950* (Harcourt, Brace and Company, Inc., 1952), p. 111. Used with permission of the publishers.

3. Evelyn Underhill, *Worship* (Torchbooks, Harper & Brothers, 1957), p. 84.

4. Rudolf Schwarz, *The Church Incarnate*, tr. by Cynthia Harris (Henry Regnery Company, 1958), pp. 11, 212.

5. Cf. Winfried Wendland, *Die Kunst der Kirche* (Lutherisches Verlagshaus, Berlin, 1953), p. 77.

6. Pie Raymond Régamey, in *Problèmes de l'Art Sacré*, pp. 109, 112.

7. Robert Bretall (ed.), *A Kierkegaard Anthology* (Princeton University Press, 1947), p. 375.

8. Edward Newman Mozley, *The Theology of Albert Schweitzer* (The Macmillan Company, 1951), p. 116.

9. Haebler, *op. cit.*, p. 68.

10. Thomas Merton, *The Seven Storey Mountain* (Harcourt, Brace and Company, Inc., 1948), pp. 108 ff. Used with permission of the publishers.

11. Eduard Spranger, *Types of Men*, tr. by Paul J. W. Pigors (Niemeyer, Halle, 1928), p. 162.

12. Cf. Iris V. Cully, *The Dynamics of Christian Education* (The Westminster Press, 1958).

13. *Ibid.*, p. 55.

Chapter IV. Scope and Limits of Christian Art

1. John Piper, *British Romantic Artists* (William Collins Sons & Co., Ltd., London, 1942), p. 21.

2. Paul Romaine-Musculus, *loc cit.*, p. 87.

3. D. M. Baillie, *God Was in Christ* (Charles Scribner's Sons, 1948), p. 114.

4. John W. Dixon, Jr., " On the Possibility of a Christian Criticism of the Arts," *The Christian Scholar* (Dec., 1957), p. 305.

5. Peter Selz, *New Images of Man* (Museum of Modern Art, 1959), p. 117.

6. Barrett, *op. cit.*, p. 56.

7. Thomas Merton, *Seeds of Contemplation* (Dell Publishing Company, 1949), pp. 102 f.

8. Pie Raymond Régamey, *loc. cit.*, p. 117.

9. Betty Burroughs (ed.), *Vasari's Lives of the Artists* (Simon and Schuster, Inc., 1946), p. 167.

10. *Time* (Jan. 9, 1956), p. 40.

11. Walter Rauschenbusch, *Christianity and the Social Crisis* (The Macmillan Company, 1907), pp. 48 f.

12. Paul Tillich, *Theology of Culture* (Oxford University Press, 1959), p. 56.

13. Tom F. Driver, "The Arts and the Christian Evangel," *The Christian Scholar,* Vol. XL (Dec. 1957), p. 332.

14. Johan Huizinga, *The Waning of the Middle Ages* (Edward Arnold & Company, London, 1942), pp. 187, 189.

15. Charles R. Joy (ed.), *Albert Schweitzer: An Anthology* (Harper & Brothers, 1947), p. 82.

16. Jacques Maritain, *Art and Scholasticism,* tr. by J. J. Scanlan (Sheed & Ward, Inc., London, 1946), p. 42.

17. Amos Wilder, "Christianity and the Arts," *The Christian Scholar,* Vol. XL (Dec. 1957), p. 268.

18. Underhill, *op. cit.,* p. 173.

19. David Ross King, "Art and Matter," *Commonwealth* (April 11, 1947), p. 635.

20. Bretall, *op. cit.,* p. 408.

21. Baillie *op. cit.,* p. 112.

22. Johannes B. Lotz, S.J., *Christliche Inkarnation und heidnischer Mythos als Wurzel sakraler Kunst,* in: *La Filosofia della Arte Sacra* (ed.), Enrico Castelli (Padova, 1957), pp. 67 f.

23. Rainer Maria Rilke, *Sonnets to Orpheus,* tr. by M. D. Herter Norton (W. W. Norton & Company, Inc., 1942), p. 33.

24. Dorothy Sayers, *The Man Born to Be King* (Harper & Brothers, 1943), p. 21.

25. Sören Kierkegaard, *Purity of Heart,* tr. by Douglas V. Steere (Torchbooks, Harper & Brothers, 1956), p. 179.

26. M. A. Courturier, "Religious Art and the Modern Artist," *Magazine of Art,* Vol. 44 (Nov., 1951), p. 268.

Chapter V. THE TASK OF THE CHURCHES

1. Meyer Schapiro, "The Liberating Quality of *Avant-Garde* Art," *Art News,* Vol. 56, No. 4 (Summer, 1956), p. 42.

2. H. Richard Niebuhr, *Christ and Culture* (Harper & Brothers, 1951), p. 256.

3. Truman B. Douglass, "The Reconciliation of the Church and the Arts," *United Church Herald,* Vol. 2 (Jan. 15, 1959), pp. 5–7.

4. Alec Robertson, *Contrasts: The Arts and Religion* (S.C.M. Press, Ltd., London, 1947), pp. 117 f.

Index

Abstractionism, 38, 159 f.
Allston, 24, 108 f.
Anabaptists, 83
Anastasis, 64, 170, 183
Angelico, Fra, 114
Anglicanism, 94, 97, 188
Apocrypha, 64, 100, 146
Architecture, 52, 67, 119 ff.
Artists, 22, 152 ff., 183
Ascension, 109, 170
Audio-visual aids, 148 ff., 190
Augustine, 30, 33, 57, 72

Bach, 27, 105, 137, 160
Baillie, D., 154, 181
Baptism, 93, 132 f.
Baroque, 99, 135, 137
Barrett, W., 40 n 9, 155 n 6
Barth, K., 119
Batoni, 174
Beauty, 33 ff., 119, 183
Beckmann, 32, 118
Beethoven, 24, 105
Berdyaev, 23 f., 119
Bernard of Clairvaux, 74
Bernini, 99
Bible, 29, 36, 43, 60, 64, 72 f., 80,
    82, 96, 100, 139, 146 ff., 170 ff.,
    195 ff.
Blake, 109 f., 174
Bosch, 87
Botticelli, 85, 114
Bouguereau, 112, 177
Bréhier, 63 n 5
Brown, F. M., 114
Brunner, E., 119
Burkart, 137
Byzantine, 53, 56 ff., 136, 174,
    176, 182

Calvin, 83, 102
Calvinism, 94, 100
Campenhausen, H. von, 58 n 4
Caravaggio, 96, 100
Carrière, 116

Cassirer, 28
Cathedrals, 76, 136
Catherine of Siena, 138
Cézanne, 117
Chagall, 44, 152, 157
Children, 37, 148 ff., 183, 196
Churches, 18, 31, 42, 111 f., 123 ff.,
    157, 180, 186 ff.
Clement of Alexandria, 47
Cocteau, 123
Cole, T., 113 f.
Coleridge, 24
Constable, 152
Cope, G., 124 n 1
Copley, 108
Correggio, 173
Counter Reformation, 95
Courbet, 115
Couturier, 184
Crafts, 16 f., 22, 193, 198
Cranach, 83, 91 ff.
Crucifixi, 77 f., 81, 98
Crucifixion, 55, 65, 82, 106, 165,
    180 ff.
Cully, I., 148

Dali, 174 f.
Dante, 65
Daumier, 115
Death, 98, 180 f.
Delacroix, 115, 117, 172
Denis, M., 116 f.
Dewey, J., 30 n 6
Dixon, J., 155 n 4
Dolci, 96
Donatello, 87
Donne, 180
Douglass, T., 186, 191
Driver, T., 163
Dürer, 30 f., 87, 91 f.

Eastern Orthodoxy, 57, 71, 106,
    112, 124
Eckhart, Meister, 135
Education, Christian, 146 ff., 191 f.